50 ONE-MINUTE TIPS FOR BETTER COMMUNICATION

Phillip E. Bozek, PhD

A FIFTY-MINUTE™ SERIES BOOK

CRISP PUBLICATIONS, INC.
Menlo Park, California

50 ONE-MINUTE TIPS FOR BETTER COMMUNICATION

Phillip E. Bozek, PhD

CREDITS
Editor: **Tony Hicks**
Layout and Composition: **Interface Studio**
Cover Design: **Carol Harris**
Artwork: **Ralph Mapson**

Copyright © 1991 by Crisp Publications, Inc.
Printed in the United States of America

Distribution to the U.S. Trade:

National Book Network, Inc.
4720 Boston Way
Lanham, MD 20706
1-800-462-6420

Library of Congress Catalog Card Number 90-83474
Bozek, Phillip E.
50 One-Minute Tips for Better Communication
ISBN 1-56052-071-X

This book is printed on recyclable paper with soy ink.

PREFACE

Leading and attending meetings, writing business documents, and giving presentations are some of the most important communication activities in business As a business professional, you can greatly enhance your own and your organization's success by improving your skills in these three areas.

Meetings. Literally millions of business meetings are held every day in the United States alone. Because of the increasing prevalence of participative management and team decision-making, effective meetings have become more important than ever. And as you rise in your organization, you are almost certain to attend more meetings, so your skills as a meeting leader and participant can be keys to your success at higher levels. This book offers several strategies for improving the productivity and the teambuilding aspects of your business meetings.

Memos. Clearly documenting accomplishments and ideas is critical to your organization's progress and to your personal record of contributions. Also, *reading* business documents composes a signficant portion of many professionals' days. The best business writers write for their readers, so this book offers several techniques that will not only help you write more easily, but will also make your documents more reader-friendly.

Presentations. Some of the most important moments in your career can be the moments you stand up to present your ideas to colleagues. As Roger Ailes implies in the title of his fine book, *You Are the Message*, audiences associate the quality of your presentation technique with the quality of your ideas and your very identity as a professional. Excellent technique not only helps achieve your purposes but also enhances your professional credibility and self-esteem. This book proposes several very specific attitudes and techniques that can help you organize and deliver high-quality professional presentations.

The success of any business depends on relationships, and business relationships depend on clear communication. Clear communication depends on clear purposes, careful attention to the message, and thorough awareness of the audience—premises that underlie all three sections of this book. My goal in this book is to give you specific ideas to help your business communications become more clear and productive and, in doing so, to help your business relationships become more harmonious and satisfying.

Phillip E. Bozek, President
Communications Designs, Inc.

ABOUT THIS BOOK

You can use *50 One-Minute Tips to Better Communication* in several ways, including:

- **In-Between Reading.** Because of its organization into 50 individual tips, each of which can be read quickly, this book is ideal for occasional reading in waiting rooms, in airport terminals, and during other spare moments of your busy days.

- **An Overview.** *50 One-Minute Tips* contains several important ideas that form the basis of an effective overall approach to meetings, memos, and presentations. You can read the book as an overview of productive techniques to use in all three of these communication media.

- **An Appendix.** *50 One-Minute Tips* adds several innovative ideas beyond basic techniques and therefore can be used as a supplement to other how-to texts. In particular, this book cross-references several other Crisp publications where you can find additional information on many of the topics presented.

- **An Individual Study Tool.** Many of the 50 tips include application exercises which can be completed at your own pace.

- **A Source of Easy-to-Use Business Forms.** *50 One-Minute Tips* contains several fill-in forms which will help you plan, conduct, and evaluate meetings; brainstorm and organize memos; and prepare critical aspects of presentations. You are free to duplicate and use these forms as needed.

- **A Trainer's Aid.** If you are a trainer, you can easily adapt several of the techniques in this book to enhance your in-class presentations and facilitations.

- **Pre- or Post-Reading for Workshops and Seminars.** Again, if you are a trainer, this book provides excellent reading material you can use to supplement your workshop or seminar activities. An extensive bibliography suggests several texts for more extensive background reading.

Other uses may suggest themselves as you go through this book. Enjoy!

CONTENTS

CONTENTS (Continued)

PART 1

17 One-Minute Tips to Improve Your Meetings

BEFORE THE MEETING

The first question to ask yourself is: Is this meeting really necessary? Tips 1 and 2 will help you decide. If you go ahead with the meeting, tips 3 and 4 will help you set it up successfully.

Note: If you would like more extensive information on the topic of meetings, Crisp Publications, Inc. has published a best-selling book titled *Effective Meeting Skills* by Marion Haynes. This book may be ordered from your distributor. Call Crisp Publications at 1-800-442-7477 to locate a distributor in your area.

TIP 3:	read pages 12–13, 26–27	*Effective Meeting Skills*
TIP 4:	read pages 18–25	*Effective Meeting Skills*
TIP 5:	read pages 16–17	*Effective Meeting Skills*
TIP 7:	read page 33	*Effective Meeting Skills*

TIP 1.
THINK OF
MEETINGS AS
INVESTMENTS

One day you wonder if maybe your office could use a new fax machine—a significant expense. In your company, you wouldn't need to get any approvals or even think about it much, you'd just run right out and buy one, right? Wrong. You need to think carefully before you spend serious money.

Except when it comes to spending it on meetings. Some organizations call meetings on a moment's notice and drag them on for hours, tying up valuable time and resources—often with no thought about how expensive meetings really are. And meetings can be *very* expensive investments. Consider:

Salaries. Every person at that meeting is drawing a salary for his or her attendance.

Benefits are also being paid to each person in the meeting. Benefit packages average about 33% of salary.

Opportunity costs. The people in your meeting may have been called away from their principal duties. As Peter Drucker says, "One either meets or one works—one cannot do both at the same time." This means that, unless your meeting is an extremely good one, time and productivity are lost.

Aside from these costs, think about other meeting-cost factors: the expense of the room, rental, or depreciation on audiovisual equipment, refreshment costs, and so on. Also consider how poorly run or unnecessary meetings affect morale. Harold Reimer, a meeting productivity consultant, has estimated that the average company loses $800 per year per employee on the "meeting recovery syndrome"—the time people spend around the water cooler complaining about bad meetings.

To determine how much a typical meeting in your organization costs and whether you are paying more for your meetings than you thought, complete the exercise on the next page.

TIP 1: EXERCISE

Exercise: Are You Paying Fines for Your Company Meetings?

Does your organization pay "meeting fines"—hidden financial penalties for poorly run meetings? To find out, think of one typical meeting you've attended recently—maybe one that didn't seem very productive. Grab a calculator, and fill out the form below.

1. Length of the meeting (in hours) 1. _____

2. Number of people at the meeting 2. _____

3. **Person-hour investment:** Multiply line 1 by line 2 3. _____

4. Estimated yearly salary of an average participant 4. $_____

5. **Average hourly salary:** Divide line 4 by 2,000 5. $_____

6. **Benefits per hour:** Multiply line 5 by 4/3. 6. $_____

7. **Add opportunity cost** (revenue that a participant would have generated back on the job): Double line 6 7. $_____

8. **Total "person cost" per hour:** Multiply line 7 by line 2 8. $_____

9. **Total meeting "person cost":** Multiply line 8 by line 1 9. $_____

10. **Personnel efficiency:** Of the people at the meeting, how many were absolutely critical to the purpose of the meeting? 10. _____

11. Divide line 10 by line 2 11. _____

12. **Time efficiency:** How long (in hours) should the meeting really have taken to accomplish its purposes? Consider if the meeting started late, got off track, etc. 12. _____

13. Divide line 12 by line 1. 13. _____

14. **Total meeting efficiency:** Multiply line 11 by line 13 14. _____

15. **Total return on meeting investment:** Multiply line 9 by line 14 15. $_____

16. **Your meeting fine:** Subtract line 15 from line 9 16. $_____

Line 16 represents the money your organization loses on every typical meeting. How much do you lose yearly? Multiply line 16 by the number of meetings your organization holds per year.

The figure you get may surprise you. As you can see, meetings can be very expensive. If you're spending more than you want to on meetings, keep reading this book!

TIP 2.
THINK PURPOSES,
NOT MEETINGS

Meetings are an important aspect of business life. But many managers feel they attend far too many meetings. Studies show that marketing executives meet for an average of 21 hours a week, and CEOs spend a staggering 69% of their time in meetings. Meetings can be very expensive investments of time away from other duties. Do we really need all those meetings to get things done?

Maybe not. A way to find out is to think purposes, not meetings. Before you resort to another meeting, specify what you want to accomplish and consider what other forms of communication might accomplish your purposes. (Remember, a meeting is basically a form of communication.)

For example, do you want to get feedback on a proposal? Try a questionnaire or some phone calls. Need to give out new information? Consider voice mail, a short memo, or a poster in a prominent place. Want new ideas? Put up a large ''graffiti sheet'' asking for input. Need to hear about problems? Try 10-minute one-on-ones instead of hours with the group.

This does not mean you should cancel all meetings. Good meetings create synergy; they're indispensable to healthy business. But if you suspect you hold too many meetings, experiment with other forms of communication. If you can achieve some purposes without calling meetings, then the meetings you do call will become powerful, special events.

TIP 2: EXERCISE

> ### *Exercise:* To Meet—Or Not to Meet

Directions: Answer the following questions with a Y ("yes"), an N ("no"), or a D ("it depends") Answers at bottom of this page. Count your number of correct answers to get an idea if your meetings interfere with productivity.

Should you call a group meeting...

1. _____ If your group is not prepared for the meeting?
2. _____ To discipline one person or a few people in the group?
3. _____ To praise one person or a few people in the group?
4. _____ If you don't want input from the group?
5. _____ To make routine announcements?
6. _____ To make a very important announcement?
7. _____ On the spur of the moment (for a nonemergency)?
8. _____ If you know there's a problem but don't know what it is or who should cope with it?
9. _____ To brainstorm new ideas?
10. _____ If the subject concerns only some of the group's members?
11. _____ If key participants aren't available?
12. _____ Just because you always have meetings?
13. _____ To gain acceptance for an idea?
14. _____ To get group members acquainted with each other?
15. _____ To give the appearance of doing something?

Scoring	
14–15:	Productivity guru
12–13:	High-potential manager
10–11:	Well...OK, I guess
9 or fewer:	I'm so glad you're reading this book!

1. No. 2. No. 3. Depends. Praising a team member in public can be a wonderful reason to call a meeting, but not if the praise would embarrass the one praised or if it would alienate other group members. 4. Yes. Not. 5. No. This is one of the most common reasons for unnecessary meetings. Consider using a memo. 6. Yes. Important news, especially bad news, should be delivered person-to-person. 7. No. 8. Probably Not. 9. Yes. This is one of the best reasons to meet. 10. No. Call a special subgroup meeting instead. 11. No. Postpone the meeting. 12. No. 13. Yes. 14. Yes. If the group is new or if you have a special team-building goal. 15. No, of course not. But oddly enough, some organizations do this.

Do you disagree with some of the answers? Wonderful! That means you're thinking critically about meetings. Here's the bottom line: don't call meetings without thinking hard about alternatives. Think purposes, not meetings!

TIP 3.
FORECAST YOUR MEETINGS

I suppose you're all wondering why I've called this meeting . . .

Ever hear a meeting start out with the sentence at right? If you have, chances are the meeting that ensued was not as productive as it could have been. Why not? Meeting participants weren't prepared.

Poor Forecasting Makes Inferior Meetings

An important factor causing inefficient, unproductive meetings is lack of forecasting—giving notice beforehand about the meeting's purposes and content. If participants don't know what a meeting is for, they might come without information that would have been useful. If they haven't thought about the issues beforehand, their ideas won't be as good. If they don't know the meeting's agenda, they can't help each other stick to it, and the meeting may get off track.

Unless you as a meeting leader have some specific, good reason for doing otherwise, always let meeting participants know beforehand at least the following information:

• The purpose of the meeting
• The agenda or outline
• The outcomes expected from the meeting
• What kinds of information will be expected from them
• What they can do to prepare
• When the meeting will start *and end*

If the the meeting is formal, perhaps with a written agenda, it should be easy to forecast by sending out the agenda early (please see, copy, and freely use the ''Meeting Announcement and Agenda'' form on the next page). Even if the meeting is a quickly convened ''ad hoc'' gathering, give participants a 30-second forecast of the meeting when you invite them.

If You're a Participant—Ask!

Every person at a meeting should feel responsible for the meeting's success. So when you're invited to a meeting whose purpose is unclear, call and ask—find out what you can bring that will help that meeting work better. Remember, it's your time and your meeting, too. Make your meetings successful—know the forecast, and be prepared when you walk in.

MEETING ANNOUNCEMENT AND AGENDA

Meeting called by _____ Phone _____

Purpose(s) _____

_____

Desired Outcome(s) _____

_____

_____

Date _____ Location _____

Scheduled Time		Actual Time		Leader _____
Start	Stop	Start	Stop	Timekeeper _____
				Recorder(s) _____
				_____

GROUP MEMBERS TO ATTEND

☑	Name	Preparation Tasks

AGENDA

☑	Person(s) responsible	Topic/Activity	Finish Time

TIP 4.
USE THE ROOM TO SET
THE MEETING'S TONE

Soft spotlights accent glowing oaken walls so you sink easily into a deep leather chair and lean back, almost horizontal. Classical music surrounds you. Aquarium fish drift silently, oddly upside down in a mirror above your head. Ahhh. . . .Where are you?

Answer: Your dentist's office. Going there can be *almost* a wonderful experience, because the dentist has done a masterful job of setting a perfect ''room tone.'' Now your meetings may not exactly be like pulling teeth—but even if they are, consider the differences you can make by considering:

Rooms and Room Arrangements
In general, adults respond well to pleasant, neat, attractive meeting rooms. Come to the room early and make sure it's tidy—this gives the meeting a subliminal sense of occasion. Also, a few plants and pictures encourage comfort and creativity.

If you want lots of face-to-face interaction, use a circular or perhaps a U-shaped seating arrangement (see the next page). Use a herringbone or classroom arrangement if you want a more restrained, quiet group. Long boardroom tables can create an ''us versus them'' feel; to soften this, set the meeting leader along one long side of the table and push back the chairs for better eye contact along each side.

Furniture
To stimulate a laid-back group, push the chairs close together; you may even want to hold the meeting in a smaller room to create a pleasantly pressurized atmosphere. If you want to reduce tension in the group, provide comfortable seating and lots of room between chairs. If you want to have a very fast meeting, provide no chairs at all. Standing meetings work well for quick brainstorming (but they're not practical if you have a lot to cover).

Lighting
To stimulate creative thinking, open the curtains and let in the view and the sunlight. Use full-spectrum fluorescent lighting. For dignity and calm, use soft, indirect light.

Temperature
In general, keep the temperature in the room fairly cool—65°–71°. Set it near the low end to stimulate the group, a bit higher to calm things down. But avoid going over 75° unless you want a group nap.

Amenities
To encourage informality and chattiness, provide snacks and drinks.

Logistical Details
Use the meeting room checklist on the next page to make sure you have everything you need for the meeting. Remember the old saying: ''For want of a nail, the shoe was lost...''

ROOM ARRANGEMENTS

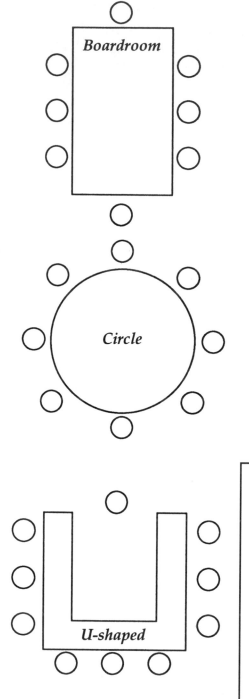

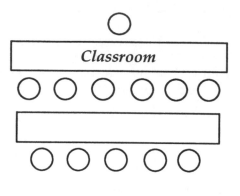

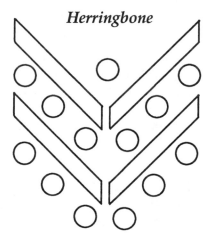

Meeting Room Checklist
For your meeting, will you need
_____ Flipcharts?
_____ Masking tape?
_____ Pushpins?
_____ A projector?
_____ A viewing screen?
_____ A whiteboard or chalkboard?
_____ Overhead, whiteboard, or flipchart markers?
_____ Chalk?
_____ Pens or pencils?
_____ Writing paper?
_____ Video or audio equipment?
_____ Name cards?
_____ Anything else?
_____ _____
_____ _____

DURING THE MEETING

You've set up the meeting. Now, how do you get people to arrive on time? By using an "odd times" strategy—see tip 5. How do you lead the meeting effectively? See tips 6–12. And how do you end the meeting with everyone feeling satisfied? By giving each participant the last word, as explained in tip 13.

Note: If you would like more extensive information on the topic of meetings, Crisp Publications, Inc. has published a best-selling book and video on *Effective Meeting Skills* by Marion Haynes. For more information on this book and video, call your local distributor or call Crisp Publications, Inc. at 1-800-442-7477 to find a distributor near you. For more information additional reading can be found in:

TIP 5:	read pages 16–17	*Effective Meeting Skills*
TIP 7:	read pages 33–34	*Effective Meeting Skills*
TIP 9:	read pages 30–31	*Effective Meeting Skills*
TIP 10:	read pages 41–45	*Effective Meeting Skills*
TIP 11:	read pages 73–74	*Effective Meeting Skills*
TIP 12:	read pages 46–50	*Effective Meeting Skills*

TIP 5.
USE AN ODD TIMES STRATEGY TO ENSURE PROMPTNESS

If you were driving along and saw this sign, what might you think? "Hmmm...that's odd...maybe the police really mean business. They've been awfully specific about the speed limit; they must mean '54.5.' I'm slowing down."

In the same way that this sign inspires notice and encourages compliance, announcing meetings that have unusual and very specific start (and finish) times may help tighten up your organization's meetings and reduce time wasted.

Do your 10:00 meetings start "10-ish"—that is, 10 or 15 minutes late? And do they start later and later each time because everyone knows everybody *else* is going to be late? Do breaks drag on indefinitely? If so, you are wasting valuable time—and perhaps morale. To solve this annoying and expensive problem, try odd times strategies at your next meeting.

For example, instead of announcing a 10:00 start time, specify 9:58 or 10:04. Specify the end of the meeting as 10:36 or 10:43. When you give breaks during longer meetings, don't just say, "Let's break for a few minutes" or even, "Let's take 15 minutes." Instead, be specific: say, "Let's break for six minutes and 45 seconds." (Incidentally, short breaks taken more frequently—at least 5 minutes every 90 minutes—tend to work better than longer breaks spaced further apart.)

When you announce these odd times, meeting participants will ask you why you're being so specific. To which you reply, "Because I mean it. Let's keep good time at this meeting." And that's a major key to the strategy—you have to mean it. The meetings must start *exactly* on the time announced, even if participants aren't all present (at first, they won't be). Breaks need to be exactly as long as planned; the meeting must end on time, or even a little early.

If you're able to set a precedent for precision, the credibility of your odd-times strategy will quickly establish itself. You'll help avoid the wasteful guessing games that people can play with ambiguous meeting schedules. People will show up on time and ready to work. And they won't doubt that your meetings, like very specific speed-limit signs, mean business.

TIP 6.
TAKE PUBLIC
CATEGORY MINUTES

Have you ever wondered what that minute taker in the back of your meeting room is really recording? Or felt concerned that something vital will be missed? After the meeting, have you ever waited for days for the minutes to be distributed, only to find them overlong, incomplete, or inaccurate? Worse yet, have you dreaded the idea that *you* might have to take the minutes?

Public Categories: Simple and Accurate

If your meetings suffer from any of these forms of "minutitus"—or if your meetings never have minutes but you wish they had—try using the public categories technique. It's very simple: as a group, select what categories of information; label flipchart pages with the categories; then ask a note taker to record the contributions to each category on the flipcharts, right in front of everyone. The benefits of this technique are several:

- **Concise completeness.** You record only what's essential.
- **Accuracy.** Everyone sees what's being recorded and can fix mistakes immediately.
- **Focus.** Discussions stay on track, without endless recycling, because everyone can see where discussions have already been.
- **Improved understanding.** Agreements, disagreements, and complex issues are more easily clarified by conveying them visually as well as verbally.
- **Quick Publication.** When the meeting is finished, simply have the flipcharts typed up and distributed. Voila! The minutes are finished.

Suggestions for Using Public Categories

1. Consider the categories of "Key Decisions" and "Action Items"—these may be all you need for most meetings. But always match categories to the meeting's purposes.
2. Encourage notetakers to record the exact words of participants. For example, don't change "need staff retreat" to "teambuilding suggestion." Abbreviating is OK, but paraphrasing may not be.
3. Take turns being notetaker, maybe even during the course of one meeting.

TIP 7.
USE "FUNNELING"
TO BRAINSTORM
IN GROUPS

"Funneling" is an extremely useful group technique which is borrowed from the world of training. Trainers need to get a lot of information exchanged clearly and quickly—which is really the goal of any business meeting. So, in your meetings, try funneling—you will find a hundred uses for this very flexible brainstorming tool. (If you're a trainer, you may recognize funneling as a streamlined version of the "nominal group technique.") Here's how you conduct funneling exercises:

FUNNELING

Purpose: Identifying and prioritizing lists of needs, concerns, opinions, or observations of participants about one issue.

Duration: 15–35 minutes.

Materials needed: Flipchart pages or transparencies, marking pens, pens and paper for participants.

How to conduct funneling:

A. Preliminaries. Decide what issue you want the group to discuss. Tell the group that they will be participating in a small-group brainstorming activity to generate a list of concerns or observations on the issue.

B. Team formation. Divide the participants into teams of two to seven people (teams of three to five people work best). Ask each team to appoint one person from the team as "brainstorm notetaker."

C. Idea generation. Ask each team to brainstorm as many ideas as they can on the issue in a specified number of minutes (four to seven minutes works well, depending on the complexity of the issue). Encourage them to work quickly, without evaluating ideas. The team notetaker records all ideas.

D. Prioritization of team data. Ask each team to choose three or four best ideas from the list they have generated. Allow them only two or three minutes.

E. Collection of data from teams. Ask a team for one of their top three ideas. Record the idea on a flipchart. Ask another team for one of their ideas and record it. Cycle through all teams, asking for only one idea at a time from each team, and asking teams to volunteer only ideas that have not already been offered and recorded.

F. Presentation of results. Announce that the flipchart represents the group's top priorities on the issue in question.

TIP 8.
USE "FAST NETWORKS" TO BRAINSTORM ON MULTIPLE ISSUES

"Fast Networks" is another way to energize your meetings—to have some fun but get things done. Fast Networks is a training/facilitation technique that easily lends itself to brainstorming and "group concern" meetings, especially about multiple issues. Fast Networks involves lots of walking around and lots of organized creativity and works best for groups of eight to 20 people.

FAST NETWORKS

Purpose: To identify needs, concerns, opinions, or observations of meeting participants about several issues.

Duration: 20–35 minutes.

Materials needed: Flipchart pages or transparencies, marking pens, pens and paper for each participant.

How to conduct fast networks:

A. Preliminaries. Decide what kind of information you want to get from the group—opinions, ideas, attitudes, or the like. Plan to have as many teams of participants as you have categories of information.

B. Team formation. Divide the participants into as many teams as there are categories of information. Try to have from two to seven people on each team; teams of three to five people work best. Tell each team they will be responsible for gathering information on their topic from the *entire group*. Tell them they must work very quickly.

C. Planning session (optional). Give each team a few minutes to devise a strategy for collecting their assigned information from the entire group.

D. Idea collection. Begin the data-collection period. Allow 5–10 minutes.

E. Summarizing data. Recall the teams and ask each team to retire to their corner, process the data, and produce a summary report on a transparency or flipchart. Give them about 10 minutes to prepare. Encourage them to work very quickly.

F. Presenting results. Allow each team about 1½ minutes to present their results.

G. Evaluation and award ceremony (optional). Ask each participant to vote for the best presentation. Tally and announce the results. Award a prize.

TIP 9.
KNOW HOW EFFECTIVE LEADERS BEHAVE

Remember Barney Fife, the nervous little deputy on the TV show *Mayberry RFD*? Was Barney a true and powerful leader of the community of Mayberry?

What do you mean "No, not really"? He had the badge, didn't he? He had the one bullet in his shirt pocket, didn't he? "Yes," you would reply, "but he didn't have respect. A badge doesn't make a leader. Just because someone is *given* authority doesn't necessarily mean he *has* it; real leadership is earned, not preordained."

And you'd be absolutely right. True leaders earn their leadership, whether of an empire or a staff meeting. So how does a person earn the status of leader? By the way he or she acts in the group. In his wonderful book *Small Group Decision Making*, B. Aubrey Fisher describes the typical behavior exhibited by individuals who emerge as the natural leaders of otherwise leaderless group discussions. Listed below are some notes on key behaviors to help you identify ways to gain, maintain, or build leadership in our organization's meetings:

WHAT DISCUSSION LEADERS DO

1. Ask questions early. Early in the discussion, natural leaders tend to solicit the views of other group members, hearing and evaluating many opinions.

2. Make frequent, short contributions to the discussion. Leaders interject frequent comments, but not necessarily lengthy ones. They may make quick suggestions for directing or changing the flow of the discussion—but their comments don't dominate the talk time of the group.

3. Give informed, objective views. Leaders do their homework on the issues. When they give their views, they are well-informed views, expressed with conviction. Leaders can identify impartially from the views of others those ideas that are most valuable.

4. Exhibit dynamic nonverbal communication. Natural leaders tend to have steady eye contact, strong and highly inflected voices (i.e., with lots of up-and-down intonation), dynamic gestures and body movements, and expressive facial animation.

Watch for these and other behaviors in the leaders you admire; practice them to increase your own "natural" leadership skills.

TIP 10.
10 KEY STATEMENTS OF EFFECTIVE MEETING LEADERS

Natural meeting leaders contribute frequent short comments to direct the flow of the meeting's discussions; here is a list of some specific phrases such leaders might use. Listen for these or similar phrases at your next meeting; the people offering them are probably doing a lot to help (i.e., lead) the group:

WHAT DISCUSSION LEADERS SAY

1. "Let's try this..." This could be a suggestion that the group try a new approach, either to a problem or to the discussion of a problem.

2. "What do you think?" A request for honest input, perhaps directed at more than one participant.

3. So what you're saying is..." An attempt to clarify what has just been said and perhaps to relate it to a previous comment.

4. "Good thought." Natural leaders are complimentary of other group members and their ideas, seldom missing an opportunity to reward contributions.

5. "Are we getting off track?" Always vigilant to control wasteful digressions, the leader asks for the group's help rather than demands it.

6. "Be nice"(or **"Be fair"** or **"Take it easy"**). An attempt to encourage diplomacy or to protect a group member from a harsh statement by another.

7. "Your turn, then yours." Natural leaders help maintain order in enthusiastic discussions by making sure everyone gets heard.

8. "So what have we decided?" Summarizing periodically during the meeting, as well as at the meeting's end, is critical to clear, productive communication.

9. "So who is going to do what by when?" If no specific action is taken as a result of the meeting, was the meeting really worthwhile?

10. "..."Silence is one of the most important responsibilities of a good meeting leader. To be effective, monitor your own talk time, and make time available fairly to all meeting participants. Especially if you supervise other participants, be careful to avoid dominating the discussion.

TIP 11.
USE A TIME OUT
SIGNAL TO GET
BACK ON TRACK

The staff meeting drags on like a fourth-rate drama. The characters are playing their usual roles: Manny D. Tails is giving long speeches on simple issues; Owen Lee Mee is ignoring the agenda and talking only about his own concerns; Thad L. Neverwork is interrupting to criticize every new idea. These undisciplined talkers may have positive intentions, but their actions have a negative effect: hours pass, and the meeting's focus is lost.

In typical internal meetings, groups will spend only 36 minutes of each hour in on-task discussion. The result is "one-hour" meetings that typically last 82 minutes—disrupting schedules, wasting time and money, and damaging the group's morale.

Here's a quick, gentle approach to the problem of wandering talk: as the meeting starts, propose a friendly signal that group members can use to flag wordy or off-the-point comments. Try a referee's time out—hands forming a "T." Or make your signal lighthearted: bring in old cracked 45s as "broken record" awards for repetitive talkers, nerf balls to toss at long-winded presenters, or white hankies to wave when the group "gives up" on a speaker. Or buy a small plastic bull to use as a trophy for irrelevance.

But for any such signal to work, the meeting leader and all group members must set a democratic tone and be willing to receive as well as call time outs. If your group can adapt a time-out signal, you'll be helping each other to stay on track and make your meetings work.

TIP 12.
USE THE F.A.S.T. FORMULA TO MANAGE "MEETING THEFT"

Meeting theft is behavior that steals time, productivity, or good will from business meetings—behaviors like talking too much or criticizing too quickly, carrying on side conversations, telling too many jokes or digressive stories, or always arriving late or unprepared. To the extent that such behaviors devalue meetings, they are forms of business thievery.

And yet the culprits themselves deserve to be treated with kindness and diplomacy, for a very important reason: most "meeting thieves" are well-intentioned people and may be completely unaware that their behaviors are counterproductive. (This charitable assessment is not always accurate, but it's usually wise to assume innocence.)

Use F.A.S.T. Diplomacy
Here's a talking technique that meeting leaders or fellow participants can use to coach a thief into more productive action:
> **Face** the problem directly
> **Acknowledge** the person and his or her good intentions
> **Suggest** a new behavior
> **Try again,** perhaps by modifying or escalating your approach

For example, suppose Hugh Moronly is always telling jokes—let's call him Hugh. Hugh *is* funny, but he's throwing the meeting off track. To manage him,
> **Face.** Look at him, smile, and say, "Hugh, let me make a suggestion..."
> **Acknowledge.** "First, you're jokes are great..."
> **Suggest.** "...and yet I still don't know what that good mind of yours really thinks about this issue. Seriously, can you tell us what you recommend?"
> **Try again.** If he persists, perhaps you get a bit tougher: "Hugh, come on now. We've had some good fun. But what's the real bottom line here?"

If these public interventions still don't work, ask Hugh if you can talk to him at a break. In private, tell him what you see him doing, how you interpret his actions, how you feel about them, and what you want him to do. Be assertive and more firm than you were in public.

Just as you would handle Hugh gently in public and more firmly in private, be sure to manage all "thefts" without inflicting public embarrassment. And remember, meeting leaders are not the only ones who manage theft. Every person at the meeting should take responsibility to help keep himself or herself, and other participants, on track and productive.

EXERCISE: TIP 12

Exercise: Experimenting with the F.A.S.T. Technique

For each of the meeting thefts listed in the left-hand column, think of what you would say to face the problem, acknowledge the person, suggest new behavior, and try again with an escalated effort. In the blank box at the bottom of the column, add an extra theft that you've seen in your organization.

Think carefully of the exact words you would use. Remember, gentleness and diplomacy are just as important as clarity and assertiveness.

TYPE OF THEFT	FACE	ACKNOWLEDGE	SUGGEST	TRY AGAIN
Chronic lateness to meetings				
Not taking part in discussions				
Giving far too much detail when talking				
Having side conversations				
Criticizing others' ideas too soon or too harshly				
Monopolizing discussions				

TIP 13.
GIVE EACH PARTICIPANT THE LAST WORD

A good way to close a meeting with a sense of satisfaction and completeness is to solicit from each participant a last word—one final brief comment, observation, or commitment.

How Last Words Benefit the Group

This variation of the round-robin discussion technique has several benefits. The last-words technique can:

- *Ensure full participation.* Even if someone has been quiet for most of the meeting, last words ensure that everyone is heard from at least once.

- *Reduce the potential for resentment or unstated agendas.* Everyone is encouraged to contribute a comment, and minority views are heard with respect.

- *Reduce the likelihood of ''groupthink.''* If the group has reached a low-quality decision or if the group thinks it has consensus but doesn't, last words provide a last chance for individuals to point out these failures.

- *Foster commitment to group decisions.* Final comments tend to be upbeat. They help team building and motivation.

- *Summarize the meeting.* Especially in training meetings, participants speaking last words tend to summarize the key points of the discussion.

Some Suggestions for Using Last Words

- *Preview the activity.* Tell participants you will be soliciting their comments.

- *Ask everyone to contribute.* Last words work best if every person speaks, not just those who may have been dominating the discussion all along.

- *Encourage candor.*

- *Consider asking for specific types of last words.* You might ask participants what decisions they liked best or what actions they will take as a result of the meeting.

- *Limit the length of comments.* A 30-second time limit works well.

- *Listen carefully.* Insist that all comments are heard with respect. Thank each contributor for his or her comment.

- *Use last words* during *meetings, too.* The technique will help make closure on one agenda item before the group moves on to the next item.

AFTER THE MEETING

What's left to do after the meeting is over? Evaluate it. Tip 14 shows two ways to do this.

Tips 15 and 16 give some strategies for handling ad hoc meetings and one-on-one meetings—especially with your boss.

And to end the section on meetings, tip 17 tells you in detail how to have the world's *worst* meetings!

Note: If you would like more extensive information on the topic of meetings, Crisp Publications, Inc. has published a best-selling book titled *Effective Meeting Skills* by Marion Haynes. To order this book contact your local distributor or call 1-800-442-7477 to find a distributor in your area. For more information additional reading can be found in:

TIP 14:	read pages 64-72	*Effective Meeting Skills*
TIP 15:	read pages 79-85	*Effective Meeting Skills*

TIP 14.
EVALUATE MEETINGS TO ENSURE PRODUCTIVITY

> *Things left uninspected begin to deteriorate.*
> —Dwight D. Eisenhower

Meetings are a significant part of most organizations' activities and therefore a significant responsibility of many professional individuals. Yet few organizations systematically evaluate their meetings, even though these organizations may be quite meticulous about evaluating other aspects of performance.

To ensure that your group's meetings are as productive as they can be and to avoid the deterioration President Eisenhower predicted, make sure you evaluate your meetings. You won't need to get feedback on every single meeting, especially if your group meets regularly—evaluating every third or fourth meeting is all you need do to monitor quality.

You may wish to use an open-ended format like the one on this page or the more specific format on the next page. Feel free to duplicate either form for future use.

MEETING EVALUATION

TO:

FROM:

DATE:

SUBJECT: Evaluation of Meeting

       Date:

       Title/Subject of meeting:

1. What was good about the meeting:

2. Suggestions for the next meeting:

MEETING EVALUATION

TO:
FROM:
DATE:
SUBJECT: Evaluation of Meeting
      Date:
      Title/Subject of meeting:

	Excellent	Good	Fair	Poor
1. Scheduling	4	3	2	1
2. Clarity of meeting purposes	4	3	2	1
3. Clarity of agenda	4	3	2	1
4. Meeting room	4	3	2	1
5. Promptness of meeting start	4	3	2	1
6. Promptness of meeting finish	4	3	2	1
7. Coverage of agenda	4	3	2	1
8. Keeping meeting on track	4	3	2	1
9. Clarity of meeting's decisions	4	3	2	1
10. Clarity of action plans	4	3	2	1
11. Fulfillment of original purposes	4	3	2	1
12. Leader's presentation	4	3	2	1
13. Other presentations	4	3	2	1
14. Attendees' preparation	4	3	2	1
15. Attendees' participation	4	3	2	1
16. Overall meeting effectiveness	4	3	2	1
17. _____	4	3	2	1
18. _____	4	3	2	1
19. _____	4	3	2	1
20. _____	4	3	2	1

Additional comments and suggestions:

TIP 15.
QUICK STRATEGIES FOR AD HOC MEETINGS

Many business meetings are informal or ad hoc meetings, called quickly and conducted without a written agenda. Although such meetings are impossible to plan in detail, many things can be done to ensure they run efficiently:

- *Consider your purposes* before you call a meeting. Are you sure you need a meeting? Will a memo or some phone calls achieve your purpose just as well?

- *Tell participants what the meeting is about* and what they should do before the meeting. If you are a participant, ask.

- *Clarify the start and adjourn times* of the meeting.

- *Limit the agenda.* You're much better off to make some progress on a few topics than no progress on many.

- *Start on time.*

- *Announce the agenda* at the meeting's start. Make a flipchart displaying the agenda.

- *Rein in digressions.*

- *Speak concisely* and encourage others to do the same.

- *Establish an open, noncritical atmosphere.*

- *Stay vigilant about the agenda and the time.* Remind your colleagues (and yourself) to stay on topic and on time.

- *Give breaks.* Try short, frequent, precisely timed breaks instead of longer, less frequent, vaguely timed breaks.

- *Periodically summarize* the progress of the meeting.

- *Clarify key decisions and action items* at the end of the meeting. Specify who has agreed to do what by when.

- *End on time*—or a little before.

TIP 16.
QUICK STRATEGIES FOR ONE-ON-ONE MEETINGS

Request and plan for a regular one-on-one meeting with your boss. Although ''ad hoc'' meetings are useful, don't depend on them for all the vital exchanges that are the life-blood of business. Instead, let regularly scheduled one-on-ones replace some of the ad hocs you have with your boss. You may both get more done.

Schedule it short and keep it short. Thirty or so minutes every week might be all you need—if you're organized before and during the meeting.

Make it ''your meeting.'' Get your boss to agree that this meeting is for your agenda. His or her issues are important, but agree to save them for team meetings or at least for another meeting. Make this meeting yours.

Follow a prioritized agenda. Have it ready and waiting. Discuss the most important items first. Don't try to cover too much: remember, better some progress on a few issues than no progress on many.

Bring solutions, not just problems. Bring clear descriptions of problems and issues you're facing—and also bring your best solution, your best alternatives for solutions, or at least your criteria for what a good solution would do. In short, help your boss answer your questions.

Speak concisely. Speak in ''sound bites.'' Give the overview, not the details—unless they are absolutely essential or your boss requests them. Remember, the boss manages the big picture, not the details.

Listen hard. Good listening is the key to communication.

Summarize at the end of the meeting. Reconfirm what decisions you and your boss have made and who is supposed to do what. Record these key decisions and action plans.

Encourage your subordinates to schedule ''their meetings'' with you. Let them speak their own agendas, just as you speak yours to your superior. At their meetings, listen a lot more than you talk.

TIP 17.
HOW TO AVOID THE WORLD'S *WORST* MEETINGS

Louis E. Goose, until recently the president and CEO of the now-defunct Doldrums, Inc., offers his secret techniques for the meetings he used to hold. Tip 17 is simply to avoid doing what Mr. Goose did before his company failed.

BEFORE THE MEETING

1. Call meetings for everything. Don't even think about whether a memo or a few phone calls would work instead. A general rule: have as many meetings as possible.

2. Invite everybody to every meeting. Then plan to make everyone stay the whole time, even if only parts of the discussion are relevant to any one person.

3. Don't tell anyone what the meeting is for. This way you can begin with ''I suppose you're all wondering why I called this meeting...''

4. Don't use an agenda. Or if you do, don't give it out beforehand. Surprise, surprise!

5. Don't worry about the meeting room. Let furniture, supplies, and audiovisual equipment take care of themselves. Assume that others will bring everything they'll need. If you end up needing anything they don't have, you can just play it by ear.

6. Show up late. This way you look stylishly busy. Besides, everyone knows that ''ten o'clock'' is really slang for ''twenty after.''

DURING THE MEETING

7. Try to cover at least 10 or 12 important items in any given meeting. Overload the group whenever possible.

8. Dominate the discussion. This is especially effective if you're the boss. Even if you're not, try to talk as much as you can about whatever you want. Ignore others' ideas.

9. Say ''Yeah, but'' often. A powerful technique to stop any newfangled rock-the-boat ''creative'' idea that horns in on your talk time.

10. Use sarcasm. If ''Yeah, but'' doesn't work, try interrupting with ridicule. Do lots of frowning, folding your arms, and looking away. As you get more confident, try raising your voice and losing your temper—this works like a charm.

11. Carry on a side conversation. Let's face it, any meeting is an excellent chance to catch up on the latest gossip.

12. Don't say anything. If you don't feel like interrupting, just be completely silent for the whole meeting. Bring a doodle pad to pass the time. Avoid all eye contact.

13. Leave things alone. If anything goes wrong with the meeting, don't fix it. Let someone else take responsibility. Protect yourself at all costs.

14. Let the meeting run on and on. Don't worry if you're way over the scheduled time. The longer the meeting, the better. Just be brave and keep going. Avoid breaks if possible.

TIP 17. (Continued)

FOLLOWING UP THE MEETING

15. Never take minutes. Or if you must, don't hurry getting them distributed.

16. Avoid summaries. At the end of a meeting, never ask ''What have we decided?'' or ''Who's going to do what?'' You're working with smart people—they'll figure it out.

17. Never evaluate your meetings. They're probably just fine as they are. Besides, do you really want to know?

GOOD LUCK!

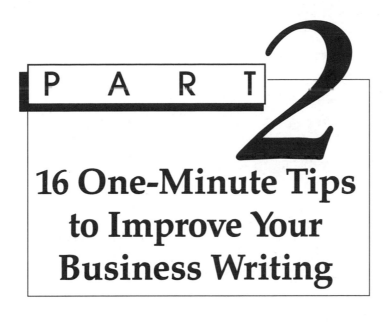

PART 2

16 One-Minute Tips to Improve Your Business Writing

GETTING STARTED

Tip 18 provides a quick test to evaluate your writing efficiency. Tips 19 and 20 show how to plan your writing with your readers in mind.

Once you've gotten started on a writing project, the next step is—get creative. Tips 21–24 guide you through two great techniques for stimulating your creativity: brainstorming and clustering. Have you ever thought of writing a cluster memo? See tip 23.

Note: If you would like more extensive information on the topic of writing, Crisp Publications, Inc., has published best-selling books titled *Technical Writing in the Corporate World* by Herman Estrin, Ph.D. and Norbert Elliot, Ph.D.; and *Better Business Writing* by Susan Brock. For more information additional reading can be found in:

TIP 18:	read pages 3–6, 16	*Technical Writing in the Corporate World*
	read page 3	*Better Business Writing*
TIP 19:	read pages 7–8, 11	*Technical Writing in the Corporate World*
TIP 20:	read page 32	*Technical Writing in the Corporate World*
	read pages 24–27	*Better Business Writing*

For more information about how to obtain these and other Crisp self-study books and videos contact your local distributor or call Crisp Publications, Inc. at 1-800-442-7477 to find a distributor in your area.

TIP 18.
HOW EFFICIENTLY DO YOU WRITE?

To find out how efficiently you write, answer the questions below about the processes you typically use when writing business memos, letters, or reports. Circle the word in the right-hand column that best describes your approach to the issues in the left-hand column. Work quickly. If you discover that any question does not apply to you, answer the question with ''sometimes.'' Scoring instructions are provided on the next page.

	A	B	C	D	E
1. Before I begin writing any business, I ask myself what my goals are for writing the document.	Always	Often	Sometimes	Seldom	Never
2. Before writing, I ask myself several questions about the readers of the document.	Always	Often	Sometimes	Seldom	Never
3. I try to write my documents perfectly the first time.	Never	Seldom	Sometimes	Often	Always
4. While writing, if I misspell a word or write an awkward phrase, I stop and fix the mistake immediately.	Never	Seldom	Sometimes	Often	Always
5. Before I write, I brainstorm and record my ideas in a rapid-fire, somewhat disorganized fashion.	Always	Often	Sometimes	Seldom	Never
6. In organizing my document, I make a special effort to group in one place all my requests for action from the reader.	Always	Often	Sometimes	Seldom	Never
7. I summarize my ideas for my readers in a clearly marked summary section.	Always	Often	Sometimes	Seldom	Never
8. The final versions of my documents have headings.	Always	Often	Sometimes	Seldom	Never
9. I use personal pronouns (*I, me, we, us, you*) in my writing.	Always	Often	Sometimes	Seldom	Never
10. I put as much information as possible onto as few pages as possible.	Never	Seldom	Sometimes	Often	Always
11. I use the formats of previously written documents as models for what I write.	Always	Often	Sometimes	Seldom	Never
12. When I revise my documents, I try to look at them only once.	Never	Seldom	Sometimes	Often	Always

TIP 18. (Continued)

Scoring Instructions. To find out how well you did on the questionnaire, count the number of responses you circled from each subcolumn on the right-hand side of the page. Then multiply that figure by the number in the "multiplier" column to get a subtotal for each subcolumn's answers. Then add the subtotals to arrive at a total score.

Subcolumn	# of Responses	Multiplier	Subtotal
A	___	×5	___
B	___	×4	___
C	___	×3	___
D	___	×2	___
E	___	×1	___

TOTAL: ___   =YOUR SCORE

Score	Rating
53–60	**Writing productivity guru.** You have very efficient writing habits. See you on the business best-seller list.
45–52	**Overachiever.** You like to write, don't you?
36–44	**Average writer.** You're doing okay, but some of your habits are slowing you down or lessening the quality of your work.
27–35	**Skill builder.** Just think how much more you're going to enjoy writing after you try some of the techniques of this book!
12–26	**Future star.** Remember, problems are opportunities!
0–11	**Can't be.** This is impossible. You must have added wrong. (Whew!) Try again.

1. Always. If you don't know exactly what your purposes are, you can't achieve them. 2. Always. Adjusting to the needs of readers is one of the most important of all writing skills. 3. Never. Write in a brainstorming way the first time; make it perfect later. 4. Never or seldom. Just circle the problems and keep writing. 5. Always (see answers to #3 and #4). 6. Always or often. In most memos, the "do" statements are what readers are really looking for. To help readers see the actions you request, group the "do's" together and label the group. 7. Always or often. Suppose readers have only 10 seconds to read your memo: will they get your message? 8. Always or often. Even in one-page documents, headings make for much easier reading. 9. Always or often. Personal pronouns clarify who does what. 10. Never or seldom. You're better off giving a reader two pages that are easy to read than one page that is tough to read. 11. Always or often. Why shouldn't you? In business, using and improving on the good ideas of others is essential—as long as you gave proper credit. 12. Never or seldom. Revise two or three times quickly, looking first for format and organization, then next for conciseness, then last for details.

TIP 19.
ASK YOURSELF QUESTIONS BEFORE YOU GIVE ANSWERS

Abraham Lincoln once said, ''When I'm getting ready to reason with a man I spend one-third of the time thinking about myself—what I'm going to say—and two-thirds thinking about him and what he's going to say.'' A similar process should become part of good business writing. Carefully think about what you plan to say, and spend even a bit more time thinking about the people to whom you're going to say it.

Planning Saves Time and Effort

Planning before you write will make the writing task less difficult. And it will actually save you time—some of the decisions you write down in your planning process may become word-for-word renditions of key statements in your final memo.

Adapt the Form on the Next Page

On the next page is a form listing a few key questions you may wish to ask yourself before you write. For shorter, less complex documents, you may only need to think about a few of these questions. For longer, more complex, or more important documents, you may need to answer all the questions and perhaps even add a few of your own to meet your document's special needs. Please feel free to duplicate and adapt this form to use for planning your future documents.

Plan Writing in Writing

Always plan *in writing*, not just in your head. If you write your plans down, you'll not only remember them more clearly—you'll also be less likely to be thrown off by doing multiple projects at the same time. You can use the form to clarify assignments from supervisors. And you'll find it much easier to get back on track if you are distracted.

DOCUMENT PLANNING SHEET

1. Document title/topic: _____

2. Overall goal(s) of document: To inform _____ , to persuade _____ , to entertain _____ .

3. Specific goal(s): To _____
_____

4. Approximate length of document: _____   5. Projected completion date: _____

6. Sources of background information: _____
_____

7. Notes on format of document (paragraphs or list form? report or memo? tables and graphs included? previous successful formats? and so on) _____
_____

8. The main point the readers will know after reading the document is: _____
_____
_____

9. Who are the readers of the document? _____
_____

10. Of all the readers of the document, the person(s) most critical to my goals for the document is/are: _____
_____

My Assessment of the Readers Is: **So I Will:**

11. The readers' knowledge of the topic and technical terminology is:
high __ low __ mixed __ unknown __

11. _____
_____

12. The readers' willingness to accept the ideas I present is:
high __ low __ mixed __ unknown __

12. _____
_____

13. The readers' opinion of me or my previous work is:
high __ low __ mixed __ unknown __

13. _____
_____

14. After reading the document, the action(s) I want the readers to take is/are: __
_____
_____

14. _____
_____

15. The readers have the following special needs or concerns: _____
_____

15. _____
_____

TIP 20.
AVOID THE "SPECIALIST'S FALLACY"

As you plan and write any business document, take special care to avoid a phenomenon that has been the death of clarity in many letters, reports, and memos: the specialist's fallacy—the mistaken belief that your readers are (or ought to be) as interested in your subject matter as you are.

How to Recognize the Specialist's Fallacy

Business writers who suffer from this malady assume that all their readers:

• Are specialists in the subject matter of the document

• Will read every word of the document

• Will know what actions to take as a result of the document

With these assumptions, writers produce documents which:

• Are too long

• Contain too much technical detail

• Overuse technical jargon or specialized terms

• Do not clearly specify action requests

• Must be read in their entirety for readers to find key points

Documents written this way may be misunderstood. Worse, they may go partly or completely unread. This can lead to lost productivity, miscommunication, and mistrust.

Where the Fallacy Originates

The specialist's fallacy comes from writers misperceiving their readers. Sometimes a writer will have a bit of intellectual snobbery ("If they don't understand this report, it's their fault. I'll *make* them read every word. Maybe they'll learn something.") More often, writers underestimate their own accomplishments as specialists ("What do you mean, this report is too jargony? This stuff is simple—if I understand it, everyone understands it").

HOW TO AVOID THE SPECIALIST'S FALLACY

- Appreciate your own accomplishments. Remember, you are a specialist—most modern professionals are. Many of your readers won't know your subject as well as you do, so adjust for them.

- Think carefully about your goals for the document and the nature of your readers.

- Think: What do readers really *need* to know? What would just be *nice* for them to know?

- Write in straightforward language. Minimize technical language and jargon.

- Omit unnecessary information—or put it in an appendix for readers who want more detail.

- Use headings to facilitate skim-and-scan reading.

- Provide a summary paragraph written in common terms.

- Group your action requests in an easy-to-find section of the document. Label the section with a heading.

TIP 21.
BRAINSTORM NOW, ORGANIZE LATER

Suppose you're in a group that's meeting to plan the next company picnic. Everyone is just tossing ideas around. Jenny says, ''How about a South Sea Islands theme?'' Brian immediately says, ''That's a stupid idea.'' What happens to Jenny? She's embarrassed and becomes very quiet—no more ideas from her. Brian's comment cut a whole human mind out of the process and will probably inhibit others' contributions, too.

Early Criticism Kills the Creative Process

Few of us would be as crass as Brian. We wouldn't be so cruel to others—yet we are often that cruel to ourselves when we write. In composing a memo or report, how many of us think of an idea, write it down, and then immediately cross it off? Or worry if it's appropriate or phrased or spelled correctly? Or worse, how many of us just stare into space, not writing anything down until we think of the perfect idea?

This early criticism is one of the chief causes of writer's block and a general dislike for the writing process. It is also a costly waste of productive time.

The Brainstorming Attitude

The solution to this early criticism is to take on a whole different attitude and to work at developing your personal brainstorming skills. Brainstorming is the very rapid creation and recording of an abundance of unedited ideas. The brainstorming attitude temporarily lets perfection go for the sake of high-output creativity. It is sometimes mistrusted and often neglected, especially by technical people whose training tells them to do it right the first time. In writing, however, the perfectionist attitude can waste time. The best attitude to have when writing is to relax that perfectionism temporarily—brainstorm now, organize (and perfect) later.

BRAINSTORMING GUIDELINES

When doing any brainstorming—whether you're writing a business document, preparing a presentation, or participating in group brainstorming at a meeting—keep the following ideas in mind as part of your brainstorming attitude.

- Think energy!

- Write as fast as you can!

- Start anywhere!

- Free yourself from organization!

- Accept every idea, even weird ones!

- Record as many ideas as possible!

- Write everything down; use abbreviations!

- Ignore spelling, punctuation, sentence structure, etc.!

- Avoid all self-criticism!

- Jump freely among ideas!

- Write until you burn out; rest; repeat!

TIP 22.
TRY ''CLUSTER'' BRAINSTORMING

An excellent technique to brainstorm a new topic is to make ''cluster'' diagrams of your ideas. Clustering looks like the diagram you see below—a diagram I used to brainstorm this page. (Look carefully; you'll see virtually all the page's ideas.)

Clustering lets you work with words in a nonlinear, almost pictorial way; you create both design and language, using both your right brain and your left brain. Clustering is also very quick, and it's fun. Clustering is also interruptable—because it's nonlinear, you can easily pick up again where you left off.

How to Cluster
Write your topic in a circle in the middle of a blank page (in our example, the word ''clustering''). Radiate spokes and circles out of this center as you think of subtopics or ideas that connect to the topic. Label these new circles however you want—perhaps with the names of sections of your memo or the journalist's questions (who, what, where, why, when, how) that I used in my clustering. (In my cluster I also added a circle called ''Action Requests,'' which is a useful category to include in many business documents.)

When you cluster, work very quickly! Skip around all you want. Don't worry about neatness or even about where you record a given idea. Use a brainstorming attitude!

Action Requests
Try it! Look at the example, but don't be bound by it. Then try your own design on the next page. The next few pages have clustering blanks you can use for brainstorming or even finished ''cluster memos''!

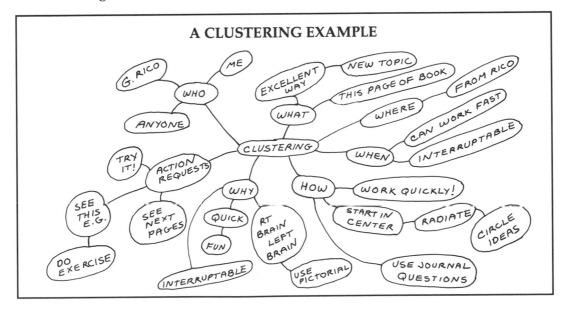

A CLUSTERING EXAMPLE

Exercise: Using Cluster Brainstorming

In the space below, brainstorm a clustering diagram of a business memo, report, or letter you need to write soon. Or, if you don't have a topic in mind, try ''What I'd do if I were in charge,'' or ''The ideal two-week vacation.''

Use any spoke and circle pattern you want. Many writers find the journalist's questions (who, what, where, when, why, how) useful to put in the first ring of circles radiating from the topic circle.

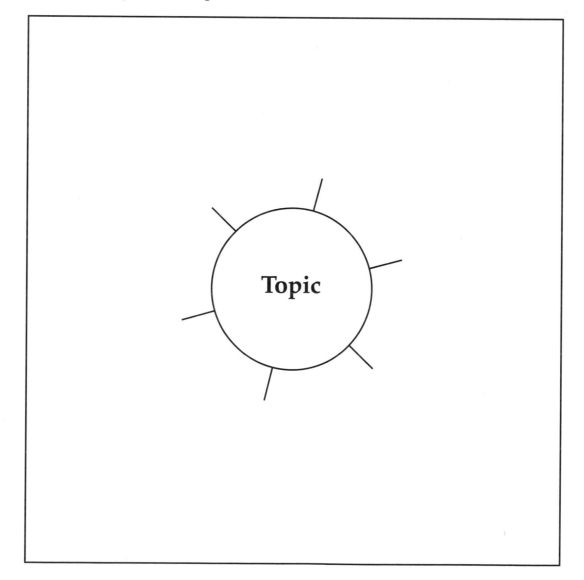

TIP 23.
TRY INTEROFFICE CLUSTER MEMOS

A unique, effective, and very quick way to send interoffice memos is to use the cluster brainstorming principle to write finished "cluster memos." I've sent and received these types of memos several times, and they can work as well as or better than conventional interoffice correspondence.

To write a cluster memo, simply create a clustering diagram and send it, just like a regular memo. Take care to write legibly and make the format of your clustering clear. Remember, this isn't just brainstorming, it's real communication. Try a predictable, reusable format like the one below, which uses the six journalist's questions and "Action Requests" as subtopic circles and a conventional "to-from-date" heading.

A Strange But Useful Technique...
Cluster memos look bizarre, but they really work. They're just as clear and communicative as regular memos, but they're very fast and easy to write because they're just like brainstorming, and they don't even require full sentences. Also, receiving cluster memos is fun; believe me, they do get read, and people look forward to your next one.

...With Some Limitations
Expect a bit of puzzlement from people the first time you try cluster memos. Explaining to them what you're up to and showing them how to do it themselves will probably help. Also, don't use cluster memos for external correspondence unless you're very sure of your readers.

AN EXAMPLE OF A CLUSTER MEMO

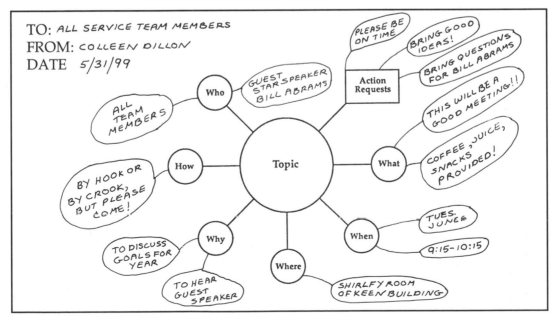

CLUSTER MEMO FORM

Duplicate and use this page as a cluster memo format.

TO:

FROM:

DATE:

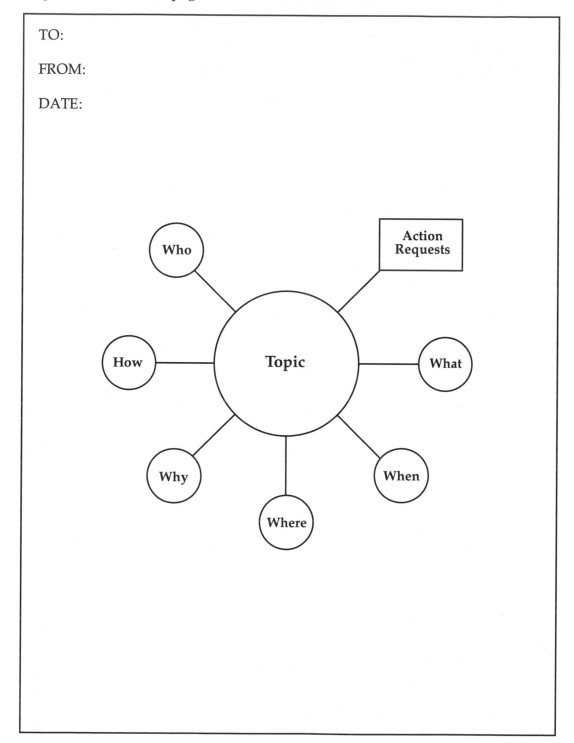

TIP 24.
FOR LONG REPORTS, USE "SECTION BRAINSTORMING"

To get started writing long reports or memos, break up the writing task into manageable chunks by using "section brainstorming."

How to Use Section Brainstorming

1. Brainstorm a list of the names of sections (or paragraphs or chapters) the report will contain. Use previous reports as models if you wish. (Having sections labeled "Summary" and "Action Requests" is usually a good idea.)

2. Use one page of paper for each section name on your brainstormed list.

3. Pick up any of these section pages, and start brainstorming the ideas that will appear in that section. Use a brainstorming attitude. Use clustering, key-word listing (as I've done in the example on this page) or any other type of brainstorming you want. Feel free to skip around among section pages as ideas occur to you.

Here's an example of section brainstorming for a memo that will be entitled "Recommendation to implement the GREATR writing process." Notice the sections are in no particular order—we're just brainstorming, not organizing yet:

Costs	_Benefits_	_Summary_	_Action Requests_	_Outline of Process_
Manuals	_Better Commun._	_Here's a process_	_Please consider_	_Goal setting_
Initial Training	_Less time writing_	_Cost/Ben.very_	_Call me_	_Reader analysis_
	Less time reading	_good_	_Authorize me_	_Energy B'storming_
	Higher prod.	_Outline below +_	_See append. for_	_Alignment (org)_
	Less Frust.	_appendix_	_more details_	_'Transmission'_
	Shorter memos	_Please consider +_		_Revising_
	Company-wide	_follow steps_		_-- Eyeballing_
	standards.			_-- Simplifying_
				-- Typo fixing

For Team Authorship, Use Flipcharts

To adapt section brainstorming to team-authorship projects, use blank flipchart pages instead of sheets of paper for report sections. Place the pages around the room and let team members wander about and add brainstorming ideas as they wish. You might also give each team member a pad of large-size sticky notes, ask them to record one idea per sticky, and stick each note on the appropriate flipchart page. Editing and arranging the team's ideas will be much easier later.

GETTING ORGANIZED

After the creative phase comes the organizing phase. Tip 25 will help you set out your memos so that your message gets across—even if the reader only scans the memo briefly.

Now comes the hard part: putting pen to paper (or fingers to the keyboard). At this stage you need all the help you can give yourself. See tip 26 on ''aerobic writing'' and tip 27 on quiet time.

Note: If you would like more extensive information on the topic of writing, Crisp Publications, Inc., has published best-selling books titled *Technical Writing in the Corporate World* by Herman Estrin, Ph.D. and Norbert Elliot, Ph.D.; *Better Business Writing* by Susan Brock; and *Writing Fitness* by Jack Swensen. For more information additional reading can be found in:

| TIP 25: | read pages 25–59 | *Technical Writing in the Corporate World* |

TIP 25.
PUT FIRST THINGS FIRST—AND LAST

Business people don't always read every word of every memo and report that crosses their desks or computer screens. Surprised? Probably not.

Like most professionals, you're probably swamped with information; you probably quickly scan incoming documents to evaluate them see how they relate to you, or to decide whether or not to study them word for word.

Would you scan the sample memo on the right? A typical sequence would start with section A, then move to section B, then E. Another typical sequence would be A,E,B.

Then, on the basis of scanning these first and last sections, you might proceed to sections C and D. Or you might put the memo down and read something else. If you don't read the rest of the memo, you're not lazy, you're just busy, and you're prioritizing on the fly.

First and Last Are Critical Locations

Busy readers tend to notice the beginnings and ends of documents. So adapt to this reader psychology. Never assume that the information you write will be read in its entirety or in the order it appears on the page. Instead, place must-see information at these strategic first and last locations on the page, and place the less important details in middle paragraphs.

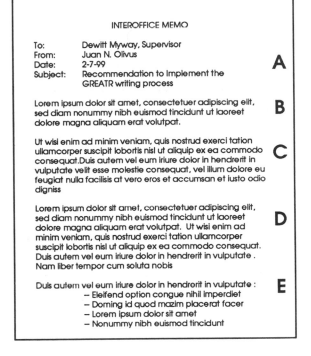

To take advantage of readers' scanning habits, try these organizing techniques:

- In the ''To-From-Date-Subject'' area, use full and informative subject lines.
- Put an executive summary, written in common terms, at position B or E.
- Put action requests—what you want the reader to do—at position E or B.
- To facilitate scanning, use headings to label each section of the document.
- Use a predictable format for your memos. For example, the format on the next page takes advantage of first and last positions and saves readers' time by giving them room to reply right on your memo.

TO:
FROM:
DATE:
SUBJECT:

SUMMARY:

THE DETAILS:

ACTION REQUESTS:

YOUR REPLY:

Feel free to duplicate and use this handy fill-in-the-blank form for your shorter memos.

TIP 26.
PRACTICE "AEROBIC WRITING"

After you have brainstormed your ideas and reorganized your brainstorming into an outline, you're ready to flesh out the sentences and paragraphs of your memo, letter, or report. Even at this stage, you should still be in a creative mood, so work quickly, although you won't be going top-speed like you did in brainstorming. If brainstorming is like sprinting, the writing you do now is like jogging or brisk walking—let's call it "aerobic writing."

Continuity is Everything

When you jog or exercise in an aerobics class, you quickly learn that continuity is important. So it is with aerobic writing. Just as you wouldn't stop in mid-jog to shower up and then start jogging again, you shouldn't stop aerobic writing to tidy up your language—not yet. Trust yourself. The good grooming will get done later, after the real workout. If you stop to perfect your writing at this stage, you'll interrupt yourself—the creative mind will defer to the editorial mind—and you may not get that creative flow back.

Some Aerobic Writing Techniques

- Use your outline as a guide.
- Make a conscious effort to keep going and avoid editing.
- If you know you've made a grammar mistake, misspelling, or if you've created an awkward phrase, just circle it, leave space for a later revision, and keep going. Don't fix it now.
- If you're handwriting, leave lots of space on the page for later revisions.
- If you're using a computer and you can touch type, consider "invisible writing"—typing with the screen either turned off or blocked by a sheet of paper—so you won't be tempted to look at and fix your writing too soon.
- If you have writer's block, try clustering your ideas. Or pretend you're talking to a buddy, saying, "The idea is simple: what I mean is..." and then talk the idea out. Then write down what you said.

Keep Going and Don't Worry

Whatever aerobic writing techniques you choose, the most important principle is *keep going and don't worry.* Give yourself a productive writing workout and plan to clean up later.

TIP 27.
INSTITUTE OFFICE QUIET TIME FOR WRITING PROJECTS

Writing business documents, like any high-concentration activity, is much easier if you can work uninterrupted. A one-minute interruption from a writing task might require as much as 20 minutes of recovery time before you can resume the flow.

But modern offices don't afford blocks of uninterrupted creative time—unless a specific quiet time is mandated as office policy: that is, a time when internal phone calls, meetings, and visits are curtailed, except for emergencies. The quiet time doesn't have to be very long—perhaps 9:30 to 10:00 on Tuesdays and Thursdays. Especially if you use brainstorming and "aerobic writing," an uninterrupted half-hour can be very productive.

Other Suggestions for Reducing Writing Distractions

Of course, the office quiet-time policy may not be practical for professionals who are on call to customers or clients or for offices in which such a policy would be difficult to coordinate. Here are a few alternative ideas for minimizing distraction:

1 **Come in early or stay late.** Go to lunch a half-hour later. Use the relatively quiet time just after noon or find the time of day when you feel most energetic, and try to find 30 minutes then.

2 **Schedule writing appointments with yourself.** If someone asks to see you during your scheduled time, say, "Sorry, I have an appointment. What other time would be good for you?"

3 **Hang up a "Do Not Disturb Until ..." or an "In Conference Until..." sign on your door.** Tell people that when your door is closed you don't want to be interrupted.

4 **Turn your writing space away from the entrance to your workspace.** Especially if you have no office door, turning away from the entrance to your office space as you write will reduce your personal interruptions.

5 **Use white noise.** In noisy open offices, get a softly playing radio or small fan to minimize distracting conversations floating over your partition.

6 **Make your office less appealing to visitors.** Sit in front of a bright window, put books on visitors' chairs, or remove visitors' chairs altogether. Be very careful when using such techniques to be especially friendly to your colleagues when you finish your writing session.

7 **Forward your calls.** Or have a secretary screen them. Or take your phone off the hook. It signals that you're busy—which you are.

8 **Promise callbacks.** If you're writing and someone calls or pops in, quickly say, ''Can I get back to you in about 15 minutes?''

9 **Find a hiding place.** Try an empty office, unoccupied conference room, or a storeroom. Or even a stall in the lavatory, or your car in the parking lot. I know professionals who boast success with both of these bizarre ''writing hiding'' places!

10 **Don't *be* an interruption.** Be sensitive to other people's need for private writing time. Be observant and flexible when balancing your needs with their time.

GETTING IT RIGHT

The last phase in producing a good piece of writing is revision. This is where you edit and improve your first draft. Tips 28–33 offer a toolkit for shaping what you've written into a document that's clear, concise, and a pleasure to read.

Note: If you would like more extensive information on the topic of writing, Crisp Publications, Inc., has published best-selling books titled *Technical Writing in the Corporate World* by Herman Estrin, Ph.D. and Norbert Elliot, Ph.D.; *Better Business Writing* by Susan Brock; and *Writing Fitness* by Jack Swensen. For more information additional reading can be found in:

TIP 29:	read pages 36–39	*Better Business Writing*
TIP 30:	read page 36	*Better Business Writing*
TIP 32:	read pages 23–46	*Writing Fitness*
	read pages 19–29, 58	*Better Business Writing*
	read page 64	*Technical Writing in the Corporate World*

TIP 28.
USE "BIG-MIDDLE-LITTLE" REVISING

Many of us have had the experience of writing a memo, sending it out without reviewing it, then seeing it later and saying "Omigosh—did *I* write *that*?" In other words, we discovered how important revising is. Without good revising, the quality of our writing skills—and by extension, the credibility of our ideas and our ability to produce good work of any kind—may be questioned by our readers.

Why Is Revising So Difficult?

Revising isn't easy, partly because writing isn't easy. Written language involves word choice, tone, punctuation, spelling, organization, connection, formality, ambiguity, visual formatting, sequence of tenses, pronoun agreement, conciseness, technical language—to name just a few. Each of these factors is an elaborate system of constantly evolving linguistic conventions.

Are we supposed to think of all that as we read through our memo one time? No way. That's why we should break up revising into manageable chunks.

To Simplify the Task: "Big-Middle-Little" Revising

The best way to revise is more than once, looking only for certain factors each time. One way to do this is to use the "big-middle-little" approach:

1. Big revising. Skim through your document, looking for the big picture—the overall content and organization of your work. Eyeball the text from a distance: does it look easy to read (with lots of marginal white space, clearly marked sections, and so on) or does it look like a brick wall of unbroken words? If a memo looks hard to read, it *is* hard to read, and it may not get read at all.

2. Middle revising. Next, quickly read for simplicity, clarity, and conciseness. Do your readers absolutely need to know everything you've written? Can you leave phrases, paragraphs, or even whole sections out? Can you simplify the language in what's left? Are your ideas clear and to the point?

3. Little revising. Next, look at the details—the grammar, spelling, and punctuation. Leave this small but very important detailing to the last. Why correct the spelling of a word you might end up eliminating?

This Book's Emphasis: Big Revising

The middle and little levels are where you're likely to get the most help from traditional style guides and from eagle-eyed colleagues. So the next few pages will focus on the often neglected "eyeball" aspects of big revising. But don't neglect any levels of revising—remember, your credibility may be on the line! And try big-middle-little revising: it's faster and more effective than trying to see everything at once.

TIP 29.
WRITE MEMO "HEADLINES" FOR INSTANT CLARITY

Imagine if today's front-page headline read only "President Bush." Or if the sports section headline said "Superbowl Score"—nothing more. "Not very informative," you'd say. "Why do I have to read the fine print to get the main point?"

We could say the same about the subject lines of many business memos. For example: "Management Meeting." What's this memo's point? Is it an invitation to a meeting? An agenda? A suggestion for the next meeting? A complaint? A request to reschedule? A background statement? You can't tell; you'd have to read the fine print. In a way, this subject line is an incomplete headline.

To help make your memos more clear, think: Subject line = Purpose + Topic. For example: "Request to Cancel Next Management Meeting. "This headline is instantly clear because it states the memo's purpose ("Request to Cancel"), then the topic ("Next Management Meeting"). Another clear one: "Summary of Revisions to Design of XYZ." Purpose: to summarize revisions. Topic: design of XYZ.

The "purpose" component of a good subject line can appear in a variety of forms: Update on, Recommendation to, Outline of, Schedule for, Proposal to, and so on. The "topic" component can refer to anything under the sun.

As one of the steps in "big revising," try combining purposes and topics in your subject lines. Doing so will help make your memos more focused, more readable—and instantly clear.

Incomplete Subject Line	**Complete Subject Line**
INTEROFFICE MEMO	INTEROFFICE MEMO
To: Dewitt Myway, Supervisor	To: Dewitt Myway, Supervisor
From: Juan N. Olivus	From: Juan N. Olivus
Date: 2-7-99	Date: 2-7-99
Subject: The GREATR writing process	**Subject: Recommendation to implement the GREATR writing process**

Exercise: Effective Subject Lines

Identify each of the subject lines below as "C" (complete—stating both purpose and topic) or "I" (incomplete—stating either purpose *or* topic). For subject lines marked "I," write in a least one way to complete the subject line. The answers are below.

_____ 1. Customer service

_____

_____ 2. Summary of regional sales figures

_____

_____ 3. Agents in Southwest rural service zones

_____

_____ 4. Office fax usage

_____

_____ 5. Recommendation to attend presentations training

_____

_____ 6. Summary of new policy on accelerating receivables

_____

_____ 7. Teamwork problems that have developed lately

_____

_____ 8. Trip report: January 11–12, 1991

_____

_____ 9. Outline of revisions to telephone installation procedures

_____

_____ 10. Complaint

_____

1. Incomplete: a topic, but no purpose. 2. Complete. 3. Incomplete. Don't be misled by how long the subject line is—it still only names a topic, not a purpose. 4. Incomplete: topic, but no purpose. 5. Complete. 6. Complete 7. Incomplete: Just as in #3, a long topic, but no purpose. 8. Complete. 9. Complete. 10. Incomplete: a purpose, but no topic. A complaint about what?

TIP 30.
ADD "BREATHING SPACE" FOR READER FRIENDLINESS

When you're revising your memo, consider adding "breathing space." Spread out the information so that it looks easy to read, so that the reader can see your ideas quickly.

Breathing Space: Two True Stories

A few years ago an old friend of mine decided to start a new life. He just picked up and moved from Chicago to Phoenix. He arrrived, wrote up a résumé—a one-pager, crammed edge-to-edge with everything he'd ever done—and started looking for work. Months went by: no job. Puzzled and worried, he revamped his résumé, spreading the same information out over two pages, making the pages breezier, much easier to read. The next week he found work.

What happened? Somebody finally read his résumé.

Another story. Once I watched an executive make a first cut of candidates for a job he was offering. He separated the résumés into three piles: "no," "maybe," and "yes." But to do so he spent less than 10 seconds looking at any one page of any résumé, judging entire professional lives that quickly.

The Bottom Line: Revise for Reader Friendliness

The moral of these stories applies to all business writing: revise your documents to look reader friendly, pleasing to the eye. Make your key information easy to find. Add breathing space with:

- **Frequent paragraph breaks.** Even use occasional one or two line paragraphs for important thoughts.

- **Lists.** Readers find listed information easier to organize, so they look at lists almost immediately. (Notice how your eyes were drawn to this list.) Lists can also condense documents by allowing the use of phrases instead of sentences.

- **Wide margins.** Readers find shorter text lines easier to read than long, edge-to-edge text lines. And wide margins let readers make marginal notes.

Remember, every business document you write is competing for readers' precious time with every other document crossing their busy desks. When you're revising your work, eyeball it, and add breathing space to make it reader friendly.

TIP 31.
USE HEADINGS TO HELP READERS PICK AND CHOOSE

As you revise your documents, consider one of the most reader-friendly of all business writing techniques: the use of headings to mark sections. Use headings even in one-page memos, and your readers will benefit in the following ways:

- **Quick overview.** Readers can scan for the main ideas.

- **Selective reading.** Readers can pick and choose the sections of the document that most interest them and set their own reading priorities.

- **Multiple-reader flexibility.** The document can appeal to readers with different levels of subject matter expertise. Technical people will find the section marked ''Technical Data,'' others may skip to ''Cost/Benefit Analysis.''

- **Breathing space.** Headings spread text out, increasing reader friendliness.

- **Easy review.** Headings allow readers to pick up the document weeks later and easily review its main ideas.

Notice the difference in readability between the memo on this page and its revision on the next page. The revision uses the techniques of a complete subject line (a memo headline), breathing space, and headings. Which would you rather read?

EXAMPLE OF A POOR LAYOUT

INTEROFFICE MEMO

To: Dewitt Myway, Supervisor
From: Juan N. Oilvus
Date: 2-7-99
Subject: The GREATR writing process

I recommend we implement The GREATR writing process in our office. The benefits we would gain are many, and the total cost of the program is minimal. The process has six relatively easy steps, which I've outlined in this memo. If you concur with my recommendation, please consider the action requests at the bottom of this page. The benefits we would receive from this program are savings of $1,500–$10,000 per year per employee; less time writing (the process would save 30%–50% of our writing time); about 25% less time reading; better communication and fewer misunderstandings among employees, resulting in higher levels of trust and better morale; higher productivity—more projects can be completed in less time; and company-wide standards by which to create and judge future documents. The costs of the program involve only manuals and initial training. Total investment per employee would be about $100. The steps include goal setting, which involves determining document purposes; reader analysis; energy brainstorming, the very rapid generation of ideas; alignment of brainstorming work into outline form; ''transmission'' of the outline into a full-sentence text; and revising, which consists of three substeps: big revising for organization and format, middle revising for conciseness and clarity, and little revising for grammar, spelling, and punctuation. Please consider this recommendation, call me if you have any questions or need more information, and authorize me to implement the process in our office.

EXAMPLE OF A BETTER LAYOUT

INTEROFFICE MEMO

To: Dewitt Myway, Supervisor
From: Juan N. Oilvus
Date: 2-7-99
Subject: Recommendation to implement The GREATR writing process

Summary

I recommend we implement The GREATR writing process in our office. The benefits we would gain are many, and the total cost of the program is minimal. The process has six relatively easy steps, which I've outlined in this memo. If you concur with my recommendation, please consider the action requests at the bottom of this page.

Benefits of the GREATR Writing Process

The benefits we would receive from this program are:

- Savings of $1,500–$10,000 per employee per year
- Less time writing. The process would save 30%–50% of our writing time.
- Less time reading. Estimated savings: 25%
- Better communication and fewer misunderstandings among employees, resulting in higher levels of trust and better morale.
- Higher productivity. More projects can be completed in less time.
- Company-wide standards by which to create and judge future documents.

Program Costs

The costs of the program involve only manuals and initial training. Total investment: about $100 per employee

Outline of the GREATR Writing Process

1. Goal setting: determining document purposes
2. Reader analysis
3. Energy brainstorming: the very rapid generation of ideas
4. Alignment of brainstorming work into outline form
5. ''Transmission'' of the outline into a full-sentence text
6. Revising, which consists of three substeps:
   —Big revising for organization and format
   —Middle revising for conciseness and clarity
   —Little revising for grammar, spelling, and punctuation.

Action Requests

Please consider this recommendation, call me if you have any questions or need more information, and authorize me to implement the process in our office.

TIP 32.
SIMPLIFY AND CLARIFY YOUR DOCUMENT

After you add headings, list, and breathing space to your document, revise it again to simplify and clarify its language. Remember that professionals don't often have time to read long or complex communications; the best business writing is clear, simple, and concise.

Some Attitudes That Will Help You Revise

To revise for simplicity and clarity, develop the attitude that the right words are the simplest words that work. Here are a few other attitudes or ways of thinking that will help you revise:

- *Avoid the specialist's fallacy.* Distinguish what readers need to know from what would merely be nice to know. Eliminate unessential ideas.

- *Write to express, not impress.* The purpose of business writing should not be to show off, but to inform. Pompous writing often alienates busy readers.

- *Write as if your readers were 12 years old.* If this sounds like odd advice, consider this quote from Albert Einstein: ''Everything should be made as simple as possible, but not simpler.''

- *Think proverbial.* Proverbs are memorable because they are short and vivid. To make your writing memorable, plan to write simple, vivid, memorable sentences rather than long, abstract dissertations.

Some Techniques That Will Help You Revise

- *Reduce or eliminate big words.* Beware of three-, four-, and five-syllable words. Change ''Our contemporary organizational structure possesses the prerequisite autonomous functioning capability'' to ''Today we have the strength we need to stand alone.'' Some technical words may be necessary. But always try to use the simplest words that work.

- *Use personal pronouns.* Instead of ''It is recommended that this procedure be implemented,'' write ''*We* recommend that *you* implement this procedure.'' Personal pronouns can help make sentences simpler, less abstract, and more personal. They also clarify the important issues of who does what.

- *There-it goes.* Reduce or eliminate unnecessary uses of *there* and *it* in phrases like ''it is,'' ''there was,'' ''it will be,'' ''there has been,'' and so on. Change ''*It is* true that *there was* anger in the crowd'' to ''The crowd was angry.''

To help make your business document as effective as possible, read through it and focus on making its language concise, simple, and clear.

TIP 32: EXERCISE

Exercise: The Bureau of Proverbs

Some government bureaucracies are famous for their use of complex jargon. Let's pretend that one such bureaucracy has performed the dubious task of rewriting some of our famous proverbs into bureaucratic style. The results of their efforts are shown below in the left-hand column.

Can you identify the original proverb that lies buried under each one of these mounds of words? Fill in your answer in the right-hand column (the first one is done for you.)

Bureaucratic Version of Proverb	**Original Proverb**
1. It is recommended that one observe with acute circumspection all visible environmental and circumstantial factors previous to a commitment to auto-induced lower-extremity acceleration.	1. *Look before you leap.*
2. Each individual cumulonimbus vaporous aqueous formation is perimetrically adorned with lustrous sterling argentite.	2. _____
3. An individual habitually procrastinating the execution of substantial activity is unavailable to specification of geographical locale.	3. _____
4. The nonspatial continuum in which events occur in apparently irreversible succession shares virtual semantic equivalence with the legally established pecuniary commodity serving as an exchangeable equivalent to all other commmodities.	4. _____

After you have filled in the correct proverb answers, do this experiment. With your hand, cover over the four bureaucratic rewrites in the left column and try to recite any one of them from memory.

Of course you couldn't do it. But now, close the book and see if you can remember any of the original proverbs in the right-hand column. You'll probably remember more than one of them—maybe even all four.

Why are proverbs memorable? Because they are clear, concise, and vivid. If you want your business writing to be memorable, keep your language short and sweet, like the language of proverbs.

2. Every cloud has a silver lining.   3. He who hesitates is lost.   4. Time is money.

TIP 33.
HOW TO COMMENT ON EACH OTHER'S WRITING

Many writers have difficulty noticing mistakes in their own writing, even if they are careful to revise. This is natural and common—knowing what you meant may blind you to what you have actually written. So some of the best resources available to writers are the opinions of their colleagues.

Yet showing your work to another person, or reviewing somebody else's work, can be an uncomfortable experience. An honest critique can be difficult to give or receive, especially since ''critique'' sounds like ''criticism,'' a word that can connote negative feedback. A better word for a review process is ''commentary,'' and a few commentary guidelines can make the process and productive.

Commentary Guidelines

Choose peer reviewers. Choose reviewers who are on your level in the organization. If you ask your superiors to review your work, you may feel their comments are orders instead of suggestions. If you ask subordinates, they may not speak honestly.

Tell reviewers what to look for. Ask commentators to be especially aware of your document's organization, or visual appeal, or conciseness, or mechanical details—whatever you feel might need most work. This makes their job easier than if you just ask them to ''look this over.''

Be helpful. When commenting on others' work, remember that your goal is to help them, not just find mistakes. Have a good heart about your task.

Speak concisely. Make your comments crisp and clean. Don't justify every comment unless the writer asks for your reasons. When you are receiving commentary, don't get defensive. Simply listen, without trying to justify your writing choices. You can decide later which review comments are valid.

Speak in compliments and suggestions. When commenting, say what you liked about the document, then make suggestions for improvements. And don't confuse suggestions with complaints: instead of saying ''I can't figure out what you mean here,'' and ''This page is too hard to read,'' say ''I suggest simplifying the language here,'' and ''You might make the margins wider and put in a heading between paragraphs 2 and 3.''

Using these guidelines will help you and your colleagues exchange constructive commentaries. You will reinforce your business relationships while you use the power of each others' eyes to make your organization's business writing more effective and productive.

PART 3

17 One-Minute Tips to Improve Your Presentations

STRUCTURING YOUR PRESENTATION

Tips 34–37 show you how to grab the audience's attention at the beginning of your presentation, how to keep it, and how to leave the audience feeling involved and enthusiastic at the end. Want to know the B.E.S.T. recipe for organizing your points? See tip 36.

Tips 38 and 39 offer suggestions for handling impromptu presentations and question-and-answer sessions ("press conferences"—tip 39).

Note: If you would like more extensive information on the topic of presentations, Crisp Publications, Inc., has published a best-selling book and video titled *Effective Presentation Skills* by Steve Mandel. Crisp, Inc. also has a book titled *Visual Aids in Business* by Claire Raines. For more information on presentations, additional reading can be found in:

TIP 34:	read page 19	*Effective Presentation Skills*
TIP 36:	read page 18	*Effective Presentation Skills*
TIP 37:	read page 23	*Effective Presentation Skills*
TIP 38:	read pages 44, 54–56	*Effective Presentation Skills*

For more information on these books and video, call your local distributor or call Crisp Publications, Inc. at 1-800-442-7477 to find a distributor in your area.

TIP 34.
EMPHASIZE BENEFITS IN YOUR INTRODUCTION

First (and last) impressions really count. Audiences tend to pay their best attention to the introductions (and the conclusions) of business presentations—so introductions and conclusions should be powerful and interesting.

Here's a tip for making your introductions memorable: *Emphasize the benefits the audience will gain by listening to you.* Make your talk obviously and immediately relevant to their concerns. Imagine that someone in your audience were to interrupt you and say, "Excuse me, Mr./Ms. Speaker, why should we listen to you? What will we gain?" The trick is to answer that question before anyone asks it.

Answer it—how? Mentioning higher profits or lower costs usually works: "In this talk are various proposals that may save us $520,000 yearly—and increase our bonuses." Or a concern: "This topic affects all of us in the following ways." Or the potential of solving a problem, or of increasing each audience member's safety, quality of life, opportunity for advancement, ability to perform, or the like.

Think carefully about your business audience's interests and concerns. Find ways your presentation will benefit your audience, and make sure they know, right from the start of your talk, what those benefits are. When you see that your audience is listening with interest, you'll more easily deliver a powerful, persuasive presentation.

Exercise: Why Should They Listen to You?

In the left column below, list some presentation topics that you plan to deliver in the near future. In the center column, identify the audience for each talk. In the right column, list the benefits the audience will gain from listening to your talk:

Topic	Audience	Benefits to Audience of Listening

TIP 35.
USE "QUICK SPECIFICS" FOR HIGH CREDIBILITY

How We Generalize about Other's Expertise

Remember that schoolteacher who wrote a few words of Latin and Greek on the board years ago? You were impressed, thinking to yourself, "Wow, Miss Fufufnik knows Latin and Greek!" Or remember when you watched a golfer hit a great tee shot on the first hole, and assumed he was an excellent golfer?

We think this way because we have a tendency to generalize from specific experiences. We tend to assume, rightly or wrongly, that behind any specific behavior is a general pattern of knowledge, skill, or similar behavior. Maybe Miss Fufufnik was trilingual, maybe she wasn't—perhaps a few words were all she knew of Latin or Greek. Maybe the golf player missed his next fifteen shots. But because we witnessed *specifics* in both cases, we assumed (at least at first) the best about both people's knowledge and skill.

In Presentations: The "Quick Specifics"

And so with professional presentations, especially persuasive ones, if you state specific names, facts, examples, statistics, stories, or analogies—especially lots of them in rapid-fire sequence—your audience is likely to assume that for each specific you gave you *could* have had more to say. They will assume that your evidence must be overwhelming, and therefore that your point must be valid.

Think "Many and Quick," instead of "Few and Deep"

Many audiences will respond best to *many* specifics *quickly* stated, as opposed to few specifics explored in depth. Audiences are generally impressed with a wide sweep, an overview of the evidence. But they may eventually require more depth. An excellent presentation strategy might be to give your wide sweep of quick specifics, and then go back and develop one of your specifics in detail. The audience will then assume that every one of your specifics could go just as deep, and they will feel a sense of the breadth *and* depth of your point, even if you don't have time to detail all your evidence.

A Final Word: Really Know the Breadth *and* the Depth of Your Evidence

The "many and quick" strategy can lead to abuses. A few bits of specific knowledge can be made to deceive unsophisticated audiences. But the best presenters really do know their material broadly *and* deeply, and are always prepared to offer fuller explanations. And the wisest audiences know that behind a presenter's quick specific evidence must lie a depth of understanding. If they have any doubts about a presenter's knowledge, they must ask for more depth, or risk being misled.

TIP 36.
USE THE B.E.S.T. RECIPE TO ORGANIZE YOUR POINTS

After you have brainstormed the specific evidence that you want to use in your speech, you need to present these specifics in an organized fashion. A very handy recipe for organizing the various points of speech is the B.E.S.T. formula: Bottom line, Evidence, Summary, Transition.

B = Bottom Line

To open each section of your speech, state in 25 words or less the point you wish to make in that section. Use a signpost phrase like ''Now my next point is...'' or ''Point #3 of my presentation is....'' This gives the audience a clear sense of where you are in your talk. Motivational speaker Leo Buscaglia provides a wonderful example of a signpost and bottom line. To open a three-minute segment of one presentation, he says: ''Another thing we have [his signpost] in this country is what I call age-ism—we're too concerned about age. It's almost sick; in fact it *is* sick [his bottom line].'' The audience now knows clearly the point he is about to support.

E = Evidence

Now list the best specific evidence, examples, statistics, stories, and analogies you have to support your point. A good technique is to signpost these specifics with a statement like ''Let me give you some examples,'' or ''Here are some statistics you may find helpful.'' To support his point on age-ism, Buscaglia tells stories about people he has met; lists actuarial statistics; draws a musical analogy; tells jokes; and mentions George Bernard Shaw, Goethe, Grandma Moses, Brooke Shields, and Jascha Heifetz—all in less than three minutes. His specific evidence is quick and convincing.

S = Summary of Bottom Line

Restate your point so the audience knows you are emerging from specifics into a general statement. You can signpost your point's summary with ''To summarize this point....'' (Do *not* say ''In conclusion'' unless you're at the end of your talk.) Buscaglia ends his age-ism point with, ''And so it isn't our bodies that are essential, our ages that are essential. There's something greater than that—there's a wondrous spirit that is eternal and that we can attach no age to. Get onto *that*!'' The audience knows clearly that he has made his point.

T = Transition to Next Point

Lead your audience to your next point with a transitional statement like, ''That leads me to the next point,'' or ''Now let's move on.''

If you clearly structure the points of your talk using the B.E.S.T. recipe—and clearly indicate where you are in your talk by using signpost statements—audiences will find your talk much easier to understand.

TIP 37.
CONCLUDE WITH OPTIMISM, CHALLENGES, AND PRONOUNS

The conclusion is an especially important part of any presentation. An ideal conclusion summarizes the main points of a presentation and also answers a very important question: ''So what?''

The best answer to ''so what'' involves translating the presentation's ideas into audience involvement. In some high-powered presentations, this may involve a dramatic rallying of the audience to action. But even in relatively low-key presentations, you may often find that an optimistic, team-building feeling would be appropriate as you conclude. To achieve this motivational effect, either in a high-key or low-key presentation, experiment with the following ideas in your conclusion:

1. **Challenge, difficulty, effort.** Tell the audience that the ideas you have proposed may not be easy to implement. Challenge them to take on the ideas anyway.

2. **Optimism.** Express as much sincere confidence as you can. Be willing to take on the challenges yourself. Predict a realistic success.

3. **The future.** Refer specifically to times to come. Even use the word *future* as you predict a brighter day.

4. **Pronouns.** Make your talk personal. Use the words *I*, *me*, or *mine*—refer to your own commitment and resolve. Tell how you feel; risk a bit of self-disclosure. Also, use the word *you* to refer to the audience—or even better, use *we*, *us*, or *our* to refer to yourself and the audience as a team.

5. **A final uplifting phrase.** Make the very last words you say turn upward, not downward. Do *not* end with a statement like, ''We will look forward to a brighter future and avoid the serious shortcomings of the past.'' Rather, say ''We will avoid the serious problems of the past and look forward to a brighter future.'' Leave the audience moving upward with your last words.

   To see how two well-known speakers have built these concluding techniques into their speeches, and to get a feel for how you might build them into the conclusions of your presentations, try the exercise on the next page.

Exercise: Analyzing Conclusions

Below are two conclusions. The first is the last few minutes of a speech given in 1984 by Geraldine Ferraro on the day she was selected to be Democratic candidate for the vice-presidency of the United States. The second is the conclusion of the last speech ever given by Martin Luther King, Jr., the day before he was assassinated.

To analyze each conclusion, find the elements of challenge, optimism, future, personal pronouns, feelings, and final uplift used by each speaker. Use the right margin to annotate your selection. To help you, these elements of Ms. Ferraro's conclusion have been marked and annotated.

Geraldine Ferraro: "In this campaign *I'm* going to take	*I*
our case for a *better future* to those Americans. I've won	*future*
their support in Queens, because they know *I'll fight for*	*challenge, effort*
them, and *I'm eager* now to win their support throughout	*"I," feelings*
the nation. When Fritz Mondale asked me to be his	
running mate, he sent a powerful signal about *the*	*future*
direction he wants to lead our country. American history is	*"we" ("our")*
about *doors being opened, doors of opportunity for everyone, as*	*optimism*
long as you're willing to earn it. The last few hours, I've got	*challenge, effort*
to tell you, I've been on the phone, talking with friends	
and supporters around the country. There's an electricity	
in the air, an excitement, *a sense of new possibilities* and of	*optimism*
pride. My good friend Charlie Rangle, congressman from	
Harlem, said to me, *"Gerry, my heart is full."* So is mine.	*"my, mine"; feelings*
Fritz Mondale knows what America is really about, and	
I'm honored to join him in this campaign for the *future.*	*"I," feelings; future; final uplift*
Thank you."	

Martin Luther King, Jr.: We've got some difficult days ahead. But that really doesn't matter with me now, because I've been to the mountain, and I don't mind. Like anyone I would like to live a long life—longevity has its place. But I'm not concerned about that now. I just want to do God's will. And He has allowed me to go up to the mountain. And I've looked over, and I've seen the promised land. I may not get there with you, but I want you to know tonight that we as a people will get to the promised land. So I'm happy tonight, I'm not worried about anything, I'm not fearing any man: mine eyes have seen the glory of the coming of the Lord.

_____
_____
_____
_____
_____
_____
_____
_____
_____
_____
_____
_____

TIP 38.
IN IMPROMPTU PRESENTATIONS, ANSWER THREE QUESTIONS

One of the greatest fears of many business people is that they may be asked to give an impromptu presentation at an important meeting. Impromptus can be very difficult to do well; speakers can stumble, ramble in a disorganized fashion—or totally blank out.

Unaccustomed as I am to public speaking . . .

Any easy and effective way to deliver impromptus is to simply ask and then answer three questions about the topic you've been given. For example, suppose the boss suddenly turns to Kathleen at a meeting and says, ''Please give us a report on what the indirect distribution department has been up to.'' She doesn't panic. She says, ''Well, the three most important questions to ask about indirect distribution are: What's the overall plan? What are the major steps in the plan? and When will the plan be completed?'' Then she simply goes back and fills in a reasonably detailed answer to each question. Then she sums up with ''That's a quick look at indirect distribution.''

Notice the structure of Kathleen's reply: she states the topic, poses all three questions, goes back to answer each one, then restates the topic.

Kathleen probably could have used any number of other questions (Who are the indirect agents? What are their sales goals? How are they doing on these goals?). Or, after she finished her three questions and answers, she could have asked the audience, ''What other questions about indirect distribution can I answer for you?'' Or, when she was first asked to speak, she might have simply asked the audience, ''Before I go off in detail on things that may or may not interest you, tell me—what questions can I answer for you?'' Then she could have followed their lead, letting the audience determine the structure of her talk.

Giving an excellent impromptu talk is no harder than asking and answering questions.

TIP 39.
TRY PRESS CONFERENCES INSTEAD OF ROUTINE PRESENTATIONS

If you give regular talks to the same group of people, experiment with a "press conference" instead of a standard presentation. The press conference is very simple and similar to the impromptu strategy: list the major sections of your talk, and take questions for a set time on each section. That's all there is to it. A press conference focuses only on what the audience really needs to hear. And it's much easier to prepare than a regular talk.

You can also make a press conference into an effective training activity by following the more elaborate steps below:

PRESS CONFERENCE

Purpose: To disseminate information from a presenter to an audience; to focus on aspects of the information that the audience will find most useful.

Duration: 20–35 minutes.

Materials needed: Four or five index cards per participant, flipchart and pens, shoeboxes (optional).

How to conduct a press conference:

A. Topic and subtopic selection. The presenter announces the topic and subtopics, writes the topic and topics on a flipchart, and (if necessary) gives a brief background statement. The presenter is allowed a maximum of 90 seconds for these activities.

B. Writing questions. Each participant quickly writes one question about each subtopic on a separate index card. The questions should be ones which the participants would like the presenter to answer.

C. Sorting questions and assigning teams. Participants drop their question cards in boxes that have subtopic labels. The presenter divides the participants into as many teams as there are subtopics.

D. Team question sorting. The presenter gives each team a shoebox of questions. Teams have a few minutes to review the questions, eliminate redundant ones, and prioritize them.

E. Questioning the presenter. The presenter selects the first team of "reporters" and directs them to ask their first question from their question cards. The presenter takes no more than one minute to answer each question (the question-asking team may interrupt the presenter if he or she is wordy or off the point). Members of the other teams listen carefully and take notes on the presenter's responses.

F. Requestioning of other teams (optional). At the end of 3–5 minutes of questioning from the first team, all other teams are allowed a short period to review their notes on the presenter's answers. The first team then asks each other team for a short summary of the presenter's points. The presenter monitors the accuracy of the summaries. The first team judges which team had the best summary.

G. Recycling. Steps E and F are repeated for each subtopic, with each team having a turn being reporters and judges.

IMPROVING YOUR NONVERBAL COMMUNICATION

It's not just what you say that's important, it's also how you say it. Tips 40–43 give some valuable ideas on improving your gestures, "voice music," eye contact, and movement.

Visual aids are an important part of many presentations. Two essential techniques are using "directory" visuals (tip 44) and creating visual-verbal cooperation (tip 45).

Note: If you would like more extensive information on the topic of presentations, Crisp Publications, Inc., has published best-selling books titled *Effective Presentation Skills* by Steve Mandel and *Visual Aids in Business* by Claire Raines. For more information additional information can be found in:

TIP 41:	read pages 49–50	*Effective Presentation Skills*
TIP 42:	read page 51	*Effective Presentation Skills*
TIP 43:	read page 52	*Effective Presentation Skills*
TIP 45:	read the entire book	*Visual Aids in Business*

TIP 40.
PRACTICE PANTOMIME TO IMPROVE YOUR GESTURES

60%–90% of the meaning of a spoken message is conveyed nonverbally—by gestures, facial expression, eye contact, movement, clothing choices, voice inflection, and so on. This striking fact indicates how important nonverbals are to a dynamic presentation.

Monitor Your Gestures

Examine your nonverbal communication. Videotape yourself giving a talk and view the tape. If you find that your gestures are unconvincing, try this unusual but very effective technique: practice delivering parts of your speech in pantomime, as if you were playing charades. Then add the words, retaining the pantomime gestures you've practiced. The resulting increase in your presentation energy can be extraordinary.

Pantomime Opportunities

''How can I pantomime a technical presentation?'' you say. ''How can I pantomime the sentence 'My department's success rates have increased'?'', trying out gestures for words and phrases. ''My'' can be gestured by touching both hands to your chest. ''Success'' could be a thumbs-up gesture, and ''increase'' could be two arms spreading out to the audience.

Gesture opportunities will appear everywhere in your talk, especially from common terms. For example, you could easily gesture the words *you, us, think, feel, before and after*, and even *divide the work into sections* while you speak them.

Listen closely for opportunities to ''play charades'' while you speak. Don't be afraid to experiment. Use your body as well as your words to express ideas. When you use 100% of your expressive ability, the result will be a wonderfully dynamic presentation.

Exercise: Using Pantomime to Increase Gestures

Think of gestures which express the concepts of the sentences below. Practice gesturing each sentence without words, then add the words. Then try the same technique with a few sentences from a presentation you'll give soon. (Key pantomime words are underlined in sentence #1.)

1. We need to *collect* ideas from *all three* sources, *throw out* the bad ones, *mold together* the good ones, and let them *grow*.
2. All of the points on the flipchart are of primary importance to all of us, and especially to me.
3. So far we've been fighting each other, or at least passing each other's ideas by. We need to start working together.

TIP 41.
USE THE ROOM TO CLARIFY THE STRUCTURE OF YOUR PRESENTATION

Readers can usually tell where they are in a book's structure—they have visual cues like chapter headings and paragraph indentations as guides. When audiences listen to presentations, however, they depend on other things for structural cues—visual aids and the presenter's signpost statements.

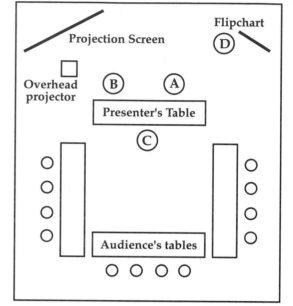

Another subtle but valuable structural cue for your audience is your movement through the presentation room. If you key your movements to various topic or subtopic shifts in your talk, your audience will receive an almost subliminal sense of an organized flow through a clearly defined structure.

Suppose you are giving a talk in the room mapped above. And suppose your talk's introductory section has four subsections: (A) you say hello, identify yourself, and name the topic of your talk; (B) you summarize your background in the subject matter; (C) you explain the benefits the audience will gain from listening; and (D) you preview the main points of your talk while referring to them on a flipchart.

You could start by delivering subsection a from location A, then move to the other locations, each movement coordinating with a subsection shift. You end at D, near the flipchart, where you forecast your points. You will have subtly signaled shifts in structure with your movements in the room.

Subliminal movement like this can be used throughout your presentation. A few ideas: (1) sit on a table or chair, maybe even among the audience members, when you want them to interact with you or with each other; (2) come toward the audience in your conclusion, delivering your last statements from position C; (3) when you're telling a story, consider walking around behind the audience as you circumnavigate the room.

Experiment with different movements, but remember: don't move pointlessly. Key your movements to the subtleties of structure, and you'll increase your own sense of dynamic movement while you help your audience understand the organization of your talk.

TIP 42.
TO IMPROVE EYE CONTACT, THINK "WHO'S THE SLEEPIEST?"

Napoleon said, "To convince a man, one must speak to his eyes." Modern studies on presentation skills agree. Good eye contact is one of the most powerful ways to retain an audience's attention.

Why? Because nonverbal communication, including the presenter's appearance, is critical to the message. When an audience observes a presenter's appearance, they look most often at the face, and in observing the face, they look most often at the eyes. So the presenter's eye contact speaks volumes.

Some Common Eye-Contact Faults

We've all seen presenters neglect the quality of their eye contact, spending too much time reading their notes or looking at their visuals. Perhaps they look above or below the audience or glance at them fleetingly, looking but not seeing. Audiences interpret the presenter's poor eye contact as lack of confidence—in himself and in his own ideas. "If he's unsure," they think, "so are we."

Ask Yourself Specific Questions

The real reason you look at the audience is to get feedback from them. You want to know how they're responding to you, so you can adjust if necessary. A way to focus on their feedback, and therefore on their faces and eyes, is to ask yourself a specific question about them—like, "Who's the sleepiest audience member?" or "Who seems to really like this talk?" or "Who needs more information?"

Practice When You're not Presenting

Practice this eye-contact question at a meeting when you're *not* presenting: look around at each person just long enough to judge how sleepy he or she is. Think about how you are looking at them, how long you dwell on each face. That's how you should be observing your audiences when you give presentations.

When you present, try to look at everybody. Don't neglect the people at the corners of the room or in that easily overlooked first row. Really observe them; try to absorb their reactions. If you observe with a specific question in mind—like "Who's the sleepiest?"—you will be communicating *with* the audiences, not *at* them. Even though only you are speaking, your presentation will become a powerful dialogue.

TIP 43.
IMITATE COMMERCIALS TO IMPROVE YOUR "VOICE MUSIC"

Did you know that when you're speaking, you're actually singing? The average speaker ranges through more than an octave of notes, just in everyday speech. You may not notice this because in speech, your notes are not usually sustained as they would be if you were singing a song. Rather, your voice slides quickly through its "music"—technically called the intonation (or inflection) of your voice.

The wider the range of intonation, the better. Sometimes the only difference between a good presenter and a boring one is the range of voice intonation. In fact, the word *monotonous* comes from mono-tone—one note. So a key to the dynamism of your voice is the musicality of your intonations.

Test Your "Voice Music"

A way to hear your voice intonations, without being distracted by your words, is to try a simple test: speak with your mouth shut. Just hum your sentences. All you'll hear is the intonation. For example, say, "Do you really think this will work?" first pronouncing the words, and then with your mouth shut, just humming the sentence.

What did you hear? A flat line with a little rise at the end? If so, your voice was boring. Or a musical roller coaster of ups and downs? If so, great! You're making voice music!

The Voice Musicians of TV and Radio

Some of the best voice musicians are broadcast announcers. Listen carefully to them, especially when they read those exciting, high-pressure ads. Ignore their words; hear their music. Some of them are wonderful: they can make any mundane product sound like the key to world happiness.

To develop your own voice music, imitate the announcers. When you're driving home or watching TV, listen to any five seconds of an announcer's voice, turn down the volume, and imitate what you heard. Try to sound exactly the same. Then turn up the volume and try again. Don't worry if your voice sounds exaggerated; remember, you're just experimenting, just play "voice music."

Exercise: Building Powerful Voice Intonations

Use the statements below to practice speaking with a wide range of voice music notes. Practice speaking each one with real feeling, real conviction. Practice humming them, too.

To increase the energy of your voice, trying punching the air with your fist as you speak. When you throw your body into a statement, your voice dynamism tends to increase.

1. I told you I don't want to be a part of it! Now leave me alone!

2. This is a bargain you absolutely can not afford to pass up! Everything—that's right, everything—is 50% off!

3. Are you kidding? You saved my life! I'll never be able to repay you!

4. We will not give up! We are going to fight this! And we are going to win!

TIP 44.
USE DIRECTORY VISUALS TO FOCUS YOUR AUDIENCE

You arrive at the presentation 15 minutes late; you don't even know what the talk is supposed to be about. You slide into your seat and look up to see the speaker and two visuals: a flipchart like the one at left and an overhead transparency like the one below.

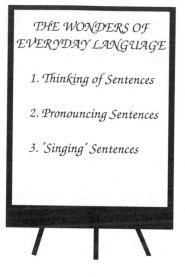

What do you know now? The talk's title is "The Wonders of Everyday Language." The talk has three parts. We're now in part 2, "Pronouncing Sentences," and part 2 has three subsections. The presenter is now discussing subsection *b*, "Articulating the Sounds."

You knew all that, without hearing any of the talk, because the presenter used a technique called directory-subdirectory visuals: displaying two or more levels of the talk's outline. (In our example, the flipchart is the directory, the transparency is a subdirectory.) When you use this technique, it's almost impossible for your audience to get lost.

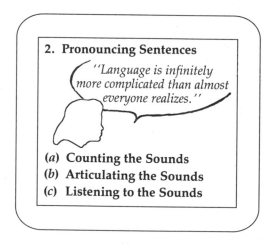

Some tips for this technique:

(1) leave your directory up for the whole talk, and change subdirectories as you move from point to point; (2) make sure that your subdirectories' titles match the language in the directory; (3) use a six-sided pencil as a pointer to lay on your transparencies. Experiment with the technique using two flipcharts, two overheads, two 35mm projectors, and so on.

If you use directory-subdirectory visuals, your audience will always know exactly where you are, even if your information is very complex, even if their attention wanders, even if they come in late.

TIP 45.
CREATE VERBAL-VISUAL COOPERATION

Using visual aids well can greatly enhance your credibility as a presenter. More importantly, using visual aids can help the audience understand, because information is coming to them through both auditory and visual channels.

Your words and visuals must cooperate, not compete, with each other. If you say one thing and display something else (especially if your visual contains words), you may be competing with your visuals, and you may be irritating, confusing, or losing your audience. To ensure that your words and your visuals cooperate:

1. **Speak what's on the visual.** If the visual contains words, speak the exact words of the visual. Avoid paraphrasing. If the visual says, ''Ethics in the Workplace,'' don't say, ''Let's talk about the best way to act on the job.'' Rather, say, ''Let's discuss ethics in the workplace.''

2. **Make sure that what they're seeing is what you're discussing.** When you're done with a visual, take it down. If you're using a flipchart, turn to a blank page; if you're using an overhead machine, turn it off.

3. **Display a visual only at the *exact moment* you start talking about it.** When you put up a visual, your audience will look at it *immediately*. If you spend even five seconds talking about something else before you go to the visual they already see, you're competing with your visual for that five seconds. (In this age of rapid-fire TV, five visual seconds is an awfully long time.)

4. **Keep the audience with you.** Because of their great visual skill, audiences will absorb a visual very quickly. If your visual contains words, they will read all the words before they listen to you. To keep them with you as you show visuals, use one of these techniques:

   • Use overlays. Build the information a little at a time, using a sequence of visuals, each of which expands on the information of the previous visual.

   • Read aloud through the entire visual. Then go back and elaborate on it.

   • Be silent, display the visual, be silent for a few seconds while the audience absorbs it, then begin your discussion.

   • Use progressive revealing. Cover parts of the visual so only the part you're discussing is visible. Reveal new sections a bit at a time, as you move on in your discussion. (Some audiences may find this technique irritating.)

Your presentations will be more effective if you keep your verbal and visual information channels cooperating.

ASKING AND ANSWERING QUESTIONS

It's often a good idea to involve the audience by asking questions. But not if your questions don't get answered. Tip 46 offers some hints on how to ask questions and how to get answers.

Often your audience will ask you questions, too. Tips 47–49 discuss how to answer questions concisely and completely—and how to hand off a question to a colleague without awkwardness.

Finally, mistakes do happen. What do you do if you find yourself in the that embarrassing situation? Don't panic—tip 50 explains how you can use mistakes to *build* your credibility.

Note: If you would like more extensive information on the topic of meetings, Crisp Publications, Inc., has published a best-selling book and video titled *Effective Presentation Skills* by Steve Mandel and an excellent book *Visual Aids in Business* by Claire Raines. For more information additional reading can be found in:

| TIP 46: | read page 54 | *Effective Presentation Skills* |
| TIP 47: | read pages 54–56 | *Effective Presentation Skills* |

TIP 46.
COUNT TO FIVE FOR BETTER AUDIENCE INVOLVEMENT

A recent study of secondary school teachers focused on how long the teachers waited after asking questions in class. How long could they tolerate the silence before they filled in the gap themselves? Answer: about one second.

If their students weren't responding, small wonder. One second is hardly enough time to answer, especially if the question is a good one. And yet the quickness of the instructor's silence filling is understandable. As anyone who presents knows, when you're up in front of people your adrenalin is pumping, and your sense of time can be distorted. Five seconds of silence can feel like 10 minutes.

Just How Long is Five Seconds?

Knowing about and adjusting to this time distortion is important. Let's experiment. Look at the second hand of your watch. Imagine yourself presenting and asking the audience a question. Then watch how long five seconds really is. Now look up; reimagine the scene, the audience, and the question, and count to five *very slowly*. That's at least as long as you should wait.

For Tough Questions, Wait Even Longer

If you ask a particularly challenging question, give your audience even longer. You may want to take some of the pressure off them while they think—instead of staring at them, look away, straighten your notes, readjust a flipchart, and then come back and say, "Well? What do you think?"

In addition to waiting long enough for answers, you'll get better audience involvement if you use these questioning tips:

- **Ask open-ended questions.** Open-ended questions are those that cannot be answered with "yes" or "no" or a one-word response. Examples of open-ended questions are: "What is your understanding of this situation?" or "What are the range of solutions to this problem?" By contrast, closed questions like "Do you agree?" or "What's the valence of uranium?" do not inspire much audience interaction.

- **Ask once and wait.** Avoid barraging the audience with multiple questions or multiple paraphrases of the same question. Don't say, "So what should we do? What is the answer? What should our responses be? There's a lot to do so what should we do first? What are our priorities? And who can help us?" Rather, say, "So what should we do?" Then wait—for at least five seconds.

TIP 47.
TO ANSWER CONCISELY, THINK "ELEVATOR SPEECH"

The elevator door opens and your boss steps in. "Hi, Sean," she says. "What's the latest on the Tracy Company deal?" You know that her office is only two floors up; you have about 15 seconds to answer. You say, "The Tracy deal looks pretty good. We have two possible orders in March with an option on a third. They'll confirm yes or no by Monday; I think it's a yes." "Good work," the boss says, stepping off the elevator. "Let me know when you get the word. See you later."

This was a sucessful exchange: a good question and a clear, concise answer. Sean's boss, like many managers and executives, likes crisp answers and respects those who can give them. A good strategy for answering questions, especially from executives, it to pretend you're in the elevator and that you have two or three floors—about 15 seconds or less—to answer. You can do it if you concentrate: think summary, think bottom line: get to the point, right now.

Sometimes, of course, you'll need a longer answer. But don't confuse thoroughness with wordiness; don't make the mistake of giving a 10-minute answer to a five-second question, unless you're absolutely sure your audience wants it. Give short, clear answers and watch your audience's reactions. You may be pleased to see that they appreciate your crisp, highly efficient "elevator" answers.

Other Tips for Answering Questions

- **Break out multiple-part questions.** If someone asks you a complex three- or four-part question, don't panic. If you can answer all the parts at once, go ahead. But a simpler approach is to answer only the first part of the question and then say, "Now, what was your second question?" Handling the questions one at a time is much easier and just as effective.

- **Always support the questioner.** Never put anyone down for asking a question, even if the question is not very good. Put-downs only make enemies. Besides, your impatience with a question may be based on a risky assumption that you've clearly presented your previous information.

  Important note: presenters can sometimes insult questioners without realizing it, by making an unintentionally hurtful comment. Suppose someone asks a question and you say, "Well, I thought I explained that, but I'll go over it again for you." Ouch!

Be kind and honest with those who ask you questions. And to make your answers clear and concise, think "elevator speech."

TIP 48.
FOR COMPLEX ANSWERS, USE THE Q-BEST-Q RECIPE

Some questions require complex answers with supporting evidence. To be most effective, these answers need to be organized in such a way that the examples and evidence support a clear, unmistakable bottom-line response. Some well-intentioned presenters, especially when discussing technical topics, make the mistake of giving detailed evidence and support *before* they speak this bottom-line summary.

If you give evidence too soon, the audience may not know if your evidence works. If they don't yet know what your evidence supports, they won't be able to evaluate it. They may even think you're being evasive.

The Q-BEST-Q Recipe

To organize longer answers, try this recipe:

1. **Q = Question repetition.** Repeat the question if the audience is large; summarize the question if the question is lengthy. Rephrase to make sure you're addressing the right issue.

   In restating the question, use either direct or indirect restatement. Direct restatement retains the question format: ''You're asking if I favor the four-day, 40-hour work week, right? My view is....'' Indirect restatement incorporates the question in the first sentence of the answer: ''With regard to the issue of the four-day, 40-hour work week, my view is...''

2. **B = Bottom-line answer.** Make it short and sweet. Aim for 25 words or less.

3. **E = Evidence.** Support your answer in a concise, rapid-fire fashion. For example: ''Let me tell you why: the four-day week will help our customers. Employee morale will go up because they'll have more days off. We'll make better use of our computer terminals. We'll suffer no loss in output. And we'll even reduce traffic jams in our parking lot.''

4. **S = Summary.** Restate the bottom-line answer, and incorporate the issue by indirectly restating the question: ''For these reasons, I believe that yes, we should have a four-day, 40-hour work week.''

5. **T = Time awareness.** Even though you've given a complex answer, think conciseness all the way through. Aim for less than a minute.

6. **Q = Questioner satisfied?** Ask the questioner, ''Have I answered your question?'' If he wants more, oblige. If he's satisfied, move on. When you check back with questioners, you can keep your answers short because the questioner can always ask you for more.

With the Q-BEST-Q recipe, you give the audience only and exactly the information they need.

TIP 48: EXERCISE

Exercise: Preparing for Complex Questions

An excellent strategy to improve your presentations is to anticipate and prepare for the more difficult questions you are likely to get from your audiences. Use the columns below to prepare Q-BEST-Q answers to the two toughest questions you're likely to get from your next audience. (For even better results, have a colleague help you think of the tough questions.) Feel free to duplicate this page to prepare for more than two questions.

Question:	Question:
Question repetition:	Question repetition:
Bottom line answer:	Bottom line answer:
Evidence or examples:	Evidence or examples:
Summary of the bottom line:	Summary of the bottom line:
Time estimate: _____	Time estimate: _____
Questioner satisfied? _____	Questioner satisfied? _____

TIP 49.
TO HAND OFF A QUESTION, USE NAME-Q-NAME

You and your colleague George have teamed up to give an important presentation to a potential client. You are in front and George is off to your side, waiting to deliver his section of the presentation. An audience member asks, ''So what should we do to upgrade our internal customer service?'' You realize that George has a better background in that area; you decide to hand off the question to George.

The Wrong Way

You say, ''George, why don't you take that one?'' George looks startled and says, ''Huh? Umm, could you— what was the question? Sorry....'' Even though George should have been paying attention, even though he *looked* like he was paying attention, he wasn't. He was thinking about his own part of the presentation (perhaps as some of us would be in the same situation). The questioner is offended, thinking no one is attending him. George looks pretty bad. So do you, because you and George are a team.

A Better Way: Name-Question-Name

Even very good team presenters will let their minds wander now and then, for reasons good or bad. So if you're handing off a question to a team member, use name-question-name. First, say George's name (everyone perks up when his name is mentioned). Then somehow repeat or rephrase the question. Then name George again and let him answer.

For example: ''George, my team member, is really more qualified to summarize what you could do to improve your internal customer service, so I'll ask him to address that. George?'' This works much better: you've gotten George's attention, given him the question and a few golden seconds to think. He answers well and looks good. So do you. The questioner is satisfied, and the audience sees you and George working together as a competent, coordinated team.

TIP 50.
USE MISTAKES TO *BUILD* YOUR CREDIBILITY

The circus lights dim; the spotlights focus on the acrobats. The ringmaster announces, ''The Soaring Lahoola Brothers will now attempt a trick performed by only seven other people in the world: the three-person triple-jacknife fingertip neck stand!'' The snare drums roll. The Lahoolas try the trick...and miss! The audience gasps. The Lahoolas try again...and miss again! The audience gasps!

But they always get it the third time, don't they? And the next night you'd see the same thing—two misses, then success. Of course, the acrobats are missing on purpose. Why? Because they know audiences will applaud their *recovery*, their courage and unflappability, perhaps even more than the trick itself. In some ways, audiencs appreciate professionalism more than perfection—coolness under fire more than no fire at all.

Presentation Mistakes Can Be Opportunities

And so with presentations. If you make an occasional mistake in your delivery—if you lose your place or put up the wrong slide—don't worry. See the moment as an opportunity to recover like a pro. Fix the mistake with a minimum of fanfare: take your time to find your place; put up the correct slide, perhaps calmly saying, ''Let's try this one.'' Then forget it and proceed. You've just improved, not hurt, your presentation.

The audience may not even notice your mistakes. If they do, they take their cues from you. If you panic, they'll be embarrassed. If you calmly recover and proceed, they think, ''Good job...nothing's going to unravel this presenter.''

Once I was giving a presentation to a brand-new client. Lots of important people were in the room. I was well into the talk—about 10 minutes—and I still couldn't get a reaction from anyone. The group seemed frozen, very nervous. I'm thinking, what's wrong? Finally a fellow in the first row holds up a little sign. It says ''Zip your pants.''

I think to myself, ''Earth, swallow me up, right now.'' I also think, ''Remember the acrobats.'' So I stood there, calmly zipped my pants, and said, ''Gosh, what do you know. That's never happened to me before. Now let's see, back to point #2....'' It wasn't easy, but I continued. At a break, two executives came up to me and said, ''Nice recovery.'' One of them added, ''But next time check your fly.''

Some Tips on Mistakes and Recoveries

Don't make mistakes on purpose. A circus act is one thing, professional communication is another. For presentations, do your homework, and always do the best you can. Audiences don't look kindly on mistakes of laziness or avoidable errors of fact.

If you make a mistake, stay calm. Think: ''Remember the acrobats,'' or ''This is an opportunity.'' Take your time—you have lots of it—to fix the mistake.

Remember: professionalism outranks perfection. If you ever saw a perfect presentation, you wouldn't like it. It'd be too slick. What audiences like is a solid effort by a real person who may be fallible, but who has the confidence to fix mistakes and continue.

BIBLIOGRAPHY

BIBLIOGRAPHY

3M Meeting Management Team. *How to Run Better Business Meetings*. New York: McGraw-Hill, 1987.

Ailes, Roger. *You Are the Message: Secrets of the Master Communicators*. Homewood, Illinois: Dow Jones–Irwin, 1988.

Allessandra, Tony, et al. *Non-Manipulative Selling*. New York: Prentice-Hall, 1987.

Applbaum, Ronald L. *Modcom: Modules in Speech Communication, Group Discussion*. Chicago: Science Research Associates, 1976.

Bacon, Terry R., and Lawrence H. Freeman. *Business Writer's Quick Reference Guide*. New York: John Wiley and Sons, 1986.

Bliss, Edwin C. *Getting Things Done*. New York: Charles Scribner's Sons, 1976.

Brinkman, Rick, and Rick Kirschner. *How to Deal with Difficult People*. Audiotape. Boulder, Colorado: Career Track Publications, 1987.

De Bono, Dr. Edward. *Six Thinking Hats*. (Audiotape) New York: International Center for Creative Thinking, 1988.

Doyle, Michael, and David Straus. *How to Make Meetings Work*. New York: Jove Books, 1982.

Drucker, Peter F. *The Effective Executive*. New York: Harper and Row, 1966.

Elbow, Peter. *Writing with Power*. New York: Oxford University Press, 1981.

Fielden, John S., and Ronald E. Dulek. *Bottom Line Business Writing*. Englewood Cliffs, New Jersey: Prentice-Hall, 1984.

Fisher, B. Aubrey. *Small Group Decision Making: Communication and the Group Process*. New York: McGraw-Hill, 1974.

Grove, Andrew S. *High Output Management*. New York: Random House, 1983.

————. *One-on-One with Andy Grove*. New York: Penguin Books, 1987.

Herrington, R. Dean. *Effective Meetings*. (Seminar).

Hon, David. *Meetings That Matter*. New York: John Wiley and Sons, 1980.

Januz, Lauren R. ''Conference Calls: Hold a Meeting over the Telephone.'' *ExecuTime* 8 (15 June 1985): p. 4.

————. ''Calling It to Order: Is This Meeting Really Necessary.'' *ExecuTime* 8 (1 August 1985): p. 4.

————. ''Focus On: During the Meeting.'' *ExecuTime* 8 (1 September 1985): pp. 2–3.

————. ''How to Be a Good Participant in a Meeting.'' *ExecuTime* 9 (15 April 1986): p. 4.

BIBLIOGRAPHY (Continued)

Jay, Anthony. "How to Run a Meeting." *Harvard Business Review* 54 (March-April 1976): pp. 43–57.

Kieffer, George David. *The Strategy of Meetings*. Audiocassette. New York: Simon and Schuster, 1988.

Lanham, Richard. *Revising Prose*. New York: Charles Scribner's Sons, 1979.

LeBouef, Michael. *Working Smart*. New York: McGraw-Hill, 1979.

Lovett, Paul D. "Meetings That Work: Plans Bosses Can Approve." *Harvard Business Review* 66 (Nov.-Dec. 1988).

Mackenzie, R. Alec. *The Time Trap*. New York: McGraw-Hill, 1972.

McVicker, Mary Frech. "Seven Ways to Make Meetings More Productive." *Piedmont Airlines* (March 1985).

Merrell, V. Dallas. *Huddling: The Informal Way to Management Success*. New York: Amacom, 1979.

Mockler, Don. *The State of Personal Productivity Research*. Salt Lake City: Franklin International Institute, 1989.

Mosvick, Roger K., and Robert B. Nelson. "We've Got to Start Meeting Like This: A Guide to Successful Business Meeting Management." *Macmillan Executive Summary Program* 3 (March 1987).

Palmer, Barbara C., and Kenneth R. Palmer. *The Successful Meeting Master Guide for Business and Professional People*. Englewood Cliffs, New Jersey: Prentice-Hall, 1983.

Prince, George M. "How to Be a Better Meeting Chairman." *Harvard Business Review* (Jan.-Feb. 1969); pp. 98–108.

Rico, Gabrielle Lusser. *Writing the Natural Way*. Los Angeles: Tarcher/Houghton Mifflin, 1983.

Thiagarajan, Sivasailam. *Committees and Meetings: Eight Strategies to Make Them More Productive*. Workshop.

————. *How to Improve Learning, Performance, and Productivity*. Workshop.

————. Timm, Paul R. *Managerial Communication*. Englewood Cliffs, New Jersey: Prentice-Hall, 1980.

Vogel, Robert A., and William D. Brooks. *Business Communication*. Menlo Park, California: Cummings Publishing Co., 1977.

Winwood, Richard I., and Hyrum W. Smith. *Excellence through Time Management*. Salt Lake City: Franklin International Institute, 1985.

NOW AVAILABLE FROM
CRISP PUBLICATIONS

Books • Videos • CD Roms • Computer-Based Training Products

If you enjoyed this book, we have great news for you. There are over 200 books available in the *50-Minute*™ Series. To request a free full-line catalog, contact your local distributor or Crisp Publications, Inc., 1200 Hamilton Court, Menlo Park, CA 94025. Our toll-free number is 800-442-7477.

Subject Areas Include:

Management

Human Resources

Communication Skills

Personal Development

Marketing/Sales

Organizational Development

Customer Service/Quality

Computer Skills

Small Business and Entrepreneurship

Adult Literacy and Learning

Life Planning and Retirement

CRISP WORLDWIDE DISTRIBUTION

English language books are distributed worldwide. Major international distributors include:

ASIA/PACIFIC

Australia/New Zealand: In Learning, PO Box 1051 Springwood QLD, Brisbane, Australia 4127
Telephone: 7-3841-1061, Facsimile: 7-3841-1580   ATTN: Messrs. Gordon

Singapore: Graham Brash (Pvt) Ltd. 32, Gul Drive, Singapore 2262
Telphone: 65-861-1336, Facsimile: 65-861-4815   ATTN: Mr. Campbell

CANADA

Reid Publishing, Ltd., Box 69559-109 Thomas Street, Oakville, Ontario Canada L6J 7R4.
Telephone: (905) 842-4428, Facsimile: (905) 842-9327   ATTN: Mr. Reid

Trade Book Stores: Raincoast Books, 8680 Cambie Street, Vancouver, British Columbia, Canada V6P 6M9.
Telephone: (604) 323–7100, Facsimile: 604-323-2600   ATTN: Ms. Laidley

EUROPEAN UNION

England: Flex Training, Ltd. 9-15 Hitchin Street, Baldock, Hertfordshire, SG7 6A, England
Telephone: 1-462-896000, Facsimile: 1-462-892417   ATTN: Mr. Willetts

INDIA

Multi-Media HRD, Pvt., Ltd., National House, Tulloch Road, Appolo Bunder, Bombay, India 400-039
Telephone: 91-22-204-2281, Facsimile: 91-22-283-6478   ATTN: Messrs. Aggarwal

MIDDLE EAST

United Arab Emirates: Al-Mutanabbi Bookshop, PO Box 71946, Abu Dhabi
Telephone: 971-2-321-519, Facsimile: 971-2-317-706   ATTN: Mr. Salabbai

SOUTH AMERICA

Mexico: Grupo Editorial Iberoamerica, Serapio Rendon #125, Col. San Rafael, 06470 Mexico, D.F.
Telephone: 525-705-0585, Facsimile: 525-535-2009   ATTN: Señor Grepe

SOUTH AFRICA

Alternative Books, Unit A3 Sanlam Micro Industrial Park, Hammer Avenue STRYDOM Park, Randburg, 2194 South Africa
Telephone: 2711 792 7730, Facsimile: 2711 792 7787   ATTN: Mr. de Haas